Copyright © 2023 by William R. Foster (Author)

All rights reserved. No part of this book may be reproduced or utilized in any form or by any means, electronic or mechanical, including photocopying, recording or by any information storage and retrieval system, without permission in writing from the publisher, except for brief quotations in critical articles or reviews.

The content of this book is based on various sources and is intended for educational and entertainment purposes only. While the author has made every effort to ensure the accuracy, completeness, and reliability of the information provided, the information may be subject to errors, omissions, or inaccuracies. Therefore, the author makes no warranties, express or implied, regarding the content of this book.

Readers are advised to seek the guidance of a licensed professional before attempting any techniques or actions outlined in this book. The author is not responsible for any losses, damages, or injuries that may arise from the use of information contained within. The information provided in this book is not intended to be a substitute for professional advice, and readers should not rely solely on the information presented.

By reading this book, readers acknowledge that the author is not providing legal, financial, medical, or professional advice. Any reliance on the information contained in this book is solely at the reader's own risk.

Thank you for selecting this book as a valuable source of knowledge and inspiration. Our aim is to provide you with insights and information that will enrich your understanding and enhance your personal growth. We appreciate your decision to embark on this journey of discovery with us, and we hope that this book will exceed your expectations and leave a lasting impact on your life.

Title: Might Unleashed: A Champion's Quest
Subtitle: Triumphs, Tragedies, and the Heart of Power

Author: William R. Foster

Table of Contents

Introduction 7
The Enigma of Might and Power 7
Racing's Timeless Icons 9
The Unbridled Spirit 11

Chapter 1: Might and Power: The Journey of a Racing Legend 13
Early Years and Training 13
First Taste of Competition 15
Signs of Greatness 17
The Road Ahead 20

Chapter 2: Gallop to Greatness: The Might and Power Story 23
The Australian Racing Scene 23
Captivating Early Races 25
Emergence of a Star 28
The Journey to 'Might' 30

Chapter 3: Thunder Down Under: The Mighty Saga of Might and Power 33
The Rise to Fame 33
The Buzz in the Racing World 36
Capturing Hearts and Headlines 39
An Era Defined 42

Chapter 4: From Birth to Glory: The Might and Power Chronicle 45
The Development of Might 45
Setting the Stage for Glory 48
Unprecedented Achievements 51
Racing's Prodigy 54

Chapter 5: Unstoppable Force: The Triumphs of Might and Power 57
Dominating the Competition 57
Breaking Records 60
The Power Within 63
Celebrations of Triumph 66

Chapter 6: Champion of the Track: The Might and Power Legacy 69
Australian Horse of the Year 69
The Spirit of a Champion 72
The Fan's Favorite 75
Beyond the Racetrack 78

Chapter 7: Caulfield to Cup: The Mighty Rise of Might and Power 80
The Caulfield Cup Triumph 80
Road to Melbourne 83
November 1997: A Historic Day 86
The Weight of Expectations 89

Chapter 8: Melbourne's Hero: The Might and Power Saga 92
The Melbourne Cup Victory 92
The Nation's Horse 95
Media Frenzy and Public Adoration 98
A Legend is Born 102

Chapter 9: Triple Crown Pursuit: Might and Power's Victorious Year 105
Conquering Major Races 105
Unforgettable Moments 109
Racing's Golden Year 113

Defying the Odds *116*

Chapter 10: Ownership Shift: The Turning Point for Might and Power **119**
A New Owner, a New Chapter *119*
Change of Fortunes *122*
Might Becomes Power *125*
Challenges on the Horizon *128*

Chapter 11: Battles and Victories: The Year of Resilience **131**
Facing Adversity *131*
The Courage to Fight *134*
The Power to Persist *137*
Hard-Won Victories *139*

Chapter 12: Guiding Light: John Wheeler and Might and Power's Journey **142**
Transition in Training *142*
Wheeler's Influence *145*
Regaining the Magic *148*
The Spirit Reborn *151*

Chapter 13: Weight of Greatness: Might and Power's Record Triumph **153**
A Record-Breaking Caulfield Cup *153*
Defying the Odds, Setting Records *156*
A Horse for the Ages *158*
The Legacy Continues *160*

Chapter 14: Horse of the Year: The Might and Power Story **162**
Australian Horse of the Year *162*
Honors and Accolades *165*

A Lasting Impact *167*
The Epitome of Might and Power *170*
Chapter 15: Farewell to Glory: The Retirement of a Racing Legend **172**
The Decision to Retire *172*
The End of an Era *175*
An Emotional Goodbye *178*
A Legacy Preserved *181*
Chapter 16: Beyond the Track: Might and Power's Legacy **184**
Life After Retirement *184*
The Impact on Racing *187*
Might's Influence *190*
A Lasting Imprint *193*
Conclusion **196**
The Legend Lives On *196*
The Unforgettable Saga *199*
The Power of Resilience *202*
Wordbook **205**
Supplementary Materials **208**

Introduction
The Enigma of Might and Power

In the world of horse racing, certain names resonate with an aura of mystique and a sense of reverence. These names transcend the boundaries of the racetrack and etch themselves into the annals of history. In the grand tapestry of racing legends, one name stands tall and proud—Might and Power. This enigmatic figure has long captured the hearts of racing enthusiasts, leaving an indelible mark on the sport's legacy.

Might and Power was more than just a racehorse; he was a force of nature. His very presence on the track sent shivers down the spines of those who witnessed his thunderous gallop. He personified the essence of power, grace, and unwavering determination. In the realm of Australian horse racing, no name echoed more profoundly than his.

This book, titled "Might Unleashed: A Champion's Quest: Triumphs, Tragedies, and the Heart of Power," seeks to unravel the enigma of Might and Power. We'll embark on a captivating journey through the life and career of this extraordinary racehorse, from his birth in New Zealand to his emergence as a racing titan on Australian soil. We'll delve into the triumphs, the tragedies, and the enduring spirit that defined this equine legend.

As we embark on this odyssey through time, one cannot help but be enchanted by the aura that surrounds Might and Power. His story is more than a chronicle of races won and records shattered; it's a testament to the indomitable spirit that drives champions to greatness. It's a story of a horse who transcended the boundaries of sport to become a symbol of resilience, courage, and the power of the heart.

The chapters that follow will paint a vivid portrait of Might and Power's journey, and you, dear reader, are about to become intimately acquainted with a legend. Prepare to be captivated as we unveil the captivating story of an equine force like no other—an enigma named Might and Power.

Racing's Timeless Icons

Horse racing, often described as the sport of kings, has a storied history that spans centuries. It's a realm where the majesty of these magnificent creatures takes center stage, and their lightning-fast sprints down the track have been captivating audiences for generations. Within this world of speed, strength, and sheer determination, certain names have risen to iconic status, transcending the boundaries of time.

Might and Power, the subject of our journey in this book, is part of this illustrious pantheon of racing's timeless icons. These are the legends whose exploits continue to be celebrated, and their stories are passed down from one generation of racing enthusiasts to the next.

While horse racing's roots extend back to ancient civilizations, it's the modern era that has seen the emergence of these indomitable stars. These icons are more than just horses; they are symbols of the sport's enduring appeal and the embodiment of what is possible when horse and rider come together in perfect harmony.

In the pages that follow, you'll find the tale of one such timeless icon, Might and Power. His journey on the track, as we'll discover, is a testament to the relentless pursuit of excellence. In exploring his life and legacy, we gain insight into not just the horse, but the sport itself. We glimpse the heights of glory and the depths of despair, the euphoria of victory and the agony of defeat, and the unwavering spirit that makes horse racing a showcase of human and equine dedication.

The history of horse racing is replete with stories of horses that became more than just champions; they became symbols of hope, inspiration, and aspiration. Might and Power is one such symbol. As we venture into the chapters that follow, we'll witness his remarkable journey and the indelible mark he left on the sport. But first, let us pay homage to the timeless icons of racing who have paved the way for a legend like Might and Power to etch his name in the annals of greatness.

The Unbridled Spirit

In the realm of horse racing, the heart of the sport beats to the rhythm of countless hooves thundering down the track. It's a world where power and grace meld into a singular, mesmerizing spectacle. Among the many racehorses that have graced this arena, one stood out with a spirit that was nothing short of unbridled—a spirit known as Might and Power.

The spirit of a racehorse transcends the track. It's the unseen force that propels these majestic creatures forward, carrying them to glory in the most prestigious races on the planet. The spirit of a champion knows no bounds. It's a force that emerges from within and propels a horse to triumph, time and time again.

Might and Power embodied this unbridled spirit in every stride. From his earliest days as a foal to his ascension to racing greatness, this horse's spirit blazed with a fire that captured the imagination of all who witnessed it. It was a spirit that inspired hope and belief, a belief that any obstacle could be overcome, any challenge met, and any rival surpassed.

In the chapters that lie ahead, we will journey through the life and career of Might and Power, a racehorse who carried the hopes and dreams of a nation. We will explore his path to glory, the races that etched his name in history, and the adversity he faced with unwavering determination.

Might and Power's unbridled spirit wasn't just about winning races. It was about resilience in the face of adversity, the courage to push beyond limits, and the ability to electrify the audience with every gallop. His spirit became a beacon of inspiration not only for racing enthusiasts but for anyone who aspires to reach the pinnacle of their chosen field.

As we delve into the chapters that follow, be prepared to witness this unbridled spirit in action. Prepare to be captivated by a force of nature that left an indelible mark on the world of horse racing. The spirit of Might and Power is a spirit that continues to inspire and ignite the hearts of all who hear its story.

Chapter 1: Might and Power: The Journey of a Racing Legend

Early Years and Training

Every legend has its origin story, and the tale of Might and Power is no exception. The journey of this remarkable racehorse began far from the thundering crowds and the adrenaline-charged atmosphere of the racetrack. It started in the quiet, serene landscapes of New Zealand, where a foal was born with the promise of greatness.

In the early years of Might and Power, the world was unaware of the force that was about to be unleashed. He was born on October 1, 1993, in the Southern Hemisphere, a time when the promise of spring was in the air. His birthplace, the renowned Wairarapa region, nestled in the heart of New Zealand's North Island, held the first chapters of his life.

As a foal, Might displayed an energy and curiosity that hinted at his future magnificence. His bloodline, a mix of New Zealand and Australian breeding, hinted at the potential coursing through his veins. It was a lineage that boasted both speed and stamina, a combination that would prove pivotal in his later success.

The formative years of a racehorse are a period of growth, exploration, and discovery. For Might and Power, it was a time of building the physical and mental foundations that would serve him in the battles to come. As he frolicked in the pastures, tested his legs in playful sprints, and engaged in the timeless dance of horsehood, his innate athleticism began to emerge.

In the chapters of this book, we will explore the influences and individuals who played pivotal roles in shaping Might and Power during his early years. From the trainers and handlers who recognized his potential to the first races that showcased his raw talent, every step of his journey will be unveiled.

Early training sessions on the tracks provided the first glimpses of his racing prowess. As he galloped and trained, it was clear that he possessed the gift of speed, and it wouldn't be long before the racing world took notice. His path to the top was far from straightforward, marked by challenges, adaptations, and relentless determination.

Join us as we step into the world of a young and spirited horse, where the foundations of his racing legend were laid. The early years and training of Might and Power represent the genesis of a journey that would take him from the tranquil pastures of New Zealand to the heart-pounding arenas of Australian horse racing.

First Taste of Competition

As Might and Power continued to mature, his innate talent for racing became increasingly apparent. It was during these formative years that he received his first taste of competition, setting the stage for a remarkable journey that would captivate the racing world.

The transition from playful foal to budding racehorse was a critical phase in the life of this extraordinary horse. It was a time of training, discipline, and the introduction to the very essence of horse racing—competition. The first foray onto the track marked the beginning of a legacy that would leave an indelible mark on Australian horse racing.

At just two years of age, Might and Power was ready to test his mettle on the racetrack. His initial forays into racing were met with a mixture of anticipation and curiosity. As he stood at the starting gates for the first time, the spectators couldn't have foreseen the greatness that was about to be unleashed.

His debut in the racing world was marked by the kind of raw talent that leaves observers in awe. It was a race where Might and Power demonstrated his natural speed and the innate ability to surge ahead of his competitors. While the result might not have been a resounding victory, it was a clear sign that something extraordinary was in the making.

As the races continued, Might and Power refined his racing skills, steadily progressing through the ranks of competition. His performances in these early races revealed a horse with a fierce competitive spirit, a determination to win, and a love for the thrill of the chase. It was evident that he was not just another racehorse; he was a force to be reckoned with.

The early competitions also exposed the racing world to a horse with a relentless work ethic and an insatiable appetite for victory. His dedication to training and racing, combined with his boundless energy, set the stage for the incredible triumphs that lay ahead.

In this chapter, we will delve into the details of Might and Power's early racing experiences, examining the races, the competition, and the gradual emergence of a true racing phenomenon. We'll explore the races that defined his early career and the moments that hinted at the greatness that was yet to come.

Might and Power's first taste of competition was just the beginning of a journey that would rewrite the record books, captivate a nation, and elevate this racehorse to legendary status. As we continue to unravel his story, we'll witness the evolution of a racing legend who left an indelible mark on the sport.

Signs of Greatness

In the world of horse racing, greatness is often recognized not in the thunderous roar of victory but in the subtle and telling signs that appear early in a horse's career. These signs, like cryptic clues, hint at the potential for immortality on the track. With Might and Power, such signs were not elusive; they were boldly evident from the beginning.

As he continued to compete and refine his skills in those early races, Might and Power displayed characteristics that set him apart. His speed was nothing short of astonishing, a raw power that seemed to defy the laws of nature. The stride that had once been the joy of his youthful gallops was now the weapon of his rivals' undoing. His explosive acceleration and ability to maintain that speed over distance hinted at a level of athleticism rarely witnessed.

But signs of greatness go beyond mere physical attributes. They encompass the intangibles, those qualities that are inherent in the hearts of champions. Might and Power exuded an unwavering determination and an indomitable spirit. He displayed a rare tenacity, an ability to dig deep and summon reserves of energy and willpower when it mattered most.

During his early years of competition, Might and Power began to cultivate a fan following. Racing enthusiasts, trainers, and jockeys all took notice of this remarkable horse. The whispers of greatness grew louder with each race, and the expectations soared to dizzying heights.

It was during this period that the media began to bestow nicknames upon Might and Power that hinted at his potential for racing supremacy. Terms like "the New Zealand dynamo" and "the force of nature" started to appear in racing reports and headlines. These were not mere titles; they were affirmations of what many believed—Might and Power was destined for something extraordinary.

Yet, it wasn't just the racetrack where Might and Power left his indelible mark. It was the hearts of those who witnessed his races, the hopes he inspired, and the awe he evoked. The signs of greatness extended beyond the track; they resonated in the collective consciousness of a nation that was falling in love with a racehorse.

In the chapters that follow, we will explore how these early signs of greatness shaped the path of Might and Power. We'll delve into the races, the moments, and the growing sense of anticipation that surrounded this extraordinary horse. It was a time when potential was transforming into reality, and the legend of Might and Power was on the cusp of being written in the annals of racing history.

The early chapters of his journey revealed a horse with the kind of promise that could only be described as extraordinary. In the next chapters, we'll watch as this promise transforms into triumphs that would set Might and Power on a trajectory toward becoming one of the greatest racehorses the world had ever seen.

The Road Ahead

As Might and Power continued to carve out a reputation as a rising star in the world of horse racing, the road ahead seemed limitless with possibilities. The promise he displayed in those early races hinted at a journey that held the potential to captivate racing enthusiasts, but no one could have predicted just how remarkable that journey would become.

The racing world was buzzing with anticipation as Might and Power advanced through his formative years. His ability to maintain a startling pace over distance and his exceptional acceleration set the stage for what promised to be an unforgettable journey. The races he won and the records he shattered were mere hints of the dominance that lay ahead.

As he navigated the road ahead, Might and Power found himself on a trajectory that few racehorses ever experience. He was entering a realm where expectations were matched only by the exhilaration of his races. Every time he stepped onto the track, the spectators were treated to a spectacle of speed and power.

The journey ahead was not without its challenges. Racing is a sport defined by both victory and defeat, and Might and Power was not exempt from facing adversity.

There were moments when he encountered rivals of formidable strength, when he bore the weight of expectations from a nation that had fallen in love with him, and when he faced the uncertainties that are an inherent part of the sport.

But the road ahead was also paved with moments of sheer brilliance. Races like the Cox Plate, where he defeated a field of outstanding competitors, and the Melbourne Cup, which catapulted him to legendary status, were milestones on this extraordinary path. His performances were not just victories; they were displays of dominance that etched his name in the annals of racing history.

The road ahead was not merely about winning races; it was about the impact Might and Power had on the sport and its enthusiasts. He became a symbol of hope, an embodiment of what is possible when talent, determination, and an unyielding spirit converge on the track. He wasn't just a racehorse; he was a force of nature that galvanized racing aficionados across Australia and beyond.

In the subsequent chapters, we will journey through the races that defined Might and Power's ascent to greatness. We'll witness the trials, the triumphs, and the unshakable spirit that propelled him forward. As we continue to unravel the chapters of his story, we'll uncover the milestones, challenges, and victories that marked this extraordinary road ahead.

Chapter 2: Gallop to Greatness: The Might and Power Story

The Australian Racing Scene

To understand the journey of Might and Power, one must first immerse themselves in the rich tapestry of the Australian racing scene. It's a world where the sport of horse racing is not just a pastime; it's a passion that courses through the veins of a nation.

Australia has a deep and storied history in horse racing. From the early days of colonial settlement, racing became a beloved tradition, one that brought communities together and captured the imagination of all who witnessed the thundering hooves and the rush to the finish line. In this country, racing isn't just a sport; it's a way of life.

The Australian racing scene is known for its diversity and depth. It's a realm where the undulating landscapes, from the sprawling outback to the lush coastal tracks, provide a canvas for races of all types. From the short, intense sprints to the grueling tests of stamina, Australian racing offers a spectrum of challenges for both horses and jockeys.

As a part of this vibrant racing scene, Might and Power found himself in a world where the competition was as fierce as the passion of the spectators. The tracks were not just surfaces for races; they were theaters of dreams, where champions were crowned and legends were made.

In this chapter, we'll explore the unique characteristics of Australian racing and the role it played in shaping the journey of Might and Power. From the iconic races that dot the calendar, such as the Melbourne Cup, the Cox Plate, and the Caulfield Cup, to the famous racecourses that bear witness to history, including Flemington, Randwick, and Moonee Valley, we'll delve into the heart of Australian racing.

The Australian racing scene was a stage that set the backdrop for Might and Power's rise to greatness. It was on these tracks, amidst the cheers of adoring fans and the pressure of intense competition, that he showcased his extraordinary talent. The spirit of Australian racing, with its traditions, legends, and unwavering devotion, became an integral part of his story.

Join us as we immerse ourselves in the world of Australian racing, a world where passion knows no bounds, and where legends like Might and Power are born. As we explore the iconic races, the revered tracks, and the fervent racing culture, we'll come to appreciate the unique essence of Australian horse racing and how it intertwined with the remarkable journey of one exceptional racehorse.

Captivating Early Races

The early races of a promising racehorse are often the moments where their true potential begins to shine through the uncertainty. For Might and Power, these early races served as a captivating prologue to a story that would soon become a legend.

As a young horse, Might and Power began to establish his reputation on the track with races that were nothing short of captivating. His debut performances hinted at a talent that was exceptional. It was a time when racing enthusiasts began to take notice, as whispers of a rising star spread through the racing world.

The charisma of Might and Power wasn't just in his remarkable speed, but in the manner in which he won races. His victories were often marked by electrifying surges in the final furlong, as he powered past his rivals with a breathtaking display of acceleration. Each win wasn't just a triumph; it was a spectacle that left spectators in awe.

One of the races that stands out during this early period was his victory in the 1996 Victoria Derby. It was a performance that left a lasting impression, as he surged ahead in the closing stages, leaving a field of talented competitors in his wake. The victory served as a prelude to what would become a remarkable year for this extraordinary racehorse.

Might and Power's captivating early races were not just about the wins; they were about the moments that hinted at his potential for greatness. His courage under pressure, his ability to maintain a relentless pace, and his capacity to handle challenging race conditions set him apart as a racehorse destined for extraordinary accomplishments.

These races were the building blocks of his racing career, marking the early stages of a journey that would captivate the hearts of racing enthusiasts. As the number of his wins began to mount, so did the anticipation and excitement of the racing world. Spectators and pundits eagerly awaited each race, wondering if the young star would continue his ascent to glory.

In the chapters that follow, we'll explore Might and Power's captivating early races in greater detail. From the Victoria Derby to the Craiglee Stakes, we'll delve into the victories and moments that made him a horse to watch. We'll witness how each race, each win, and each electrifying surge contributed to the growing legend of this extraordinary racehorse.

As we relive these early races, we'll uncover the essence of a racehorse who was not just captivating on the track, but who also captured the imagination of a nation. The captivating early races of Might and Power were more than just victories; they were the opening notes of a symphony that would echo through the annals of racing history.

Emergence of a Star

In the world of horse racing, stars are not merely born; they emerge from the ranks of the talented and the determined. Might and Power was one such star, and his ascent from a promising young racehorse to a true sensation marked the emergence of a star whose radiance would light up the Australian racing scene.

The journey to stardom for Might and Power was not a sudden burst into the limelight; it was a gradual, carefully orchestrated climb. It began with those captivating early races that hinted at his exceptional talent. As he continued to compete and win, his reputation grew, and racing enthusiasts across Australia started to take notice.

One of the pivotal moments in his emergence was the 1997 Caulfield Cup. It was in this race that Might and Power showcased his brilliance, defeating a field of esteemed competitors with ease. The manner in which he surged ahead in the final furlong left no doubt that a star was on the rise. The Caulfield Cup victory was a statement, a declaration that he was destined for greatness.

As his victories continued to accumulate, so did the expectations. Racing enthusiasts were no longer whispering about a rising star; they were proclaiming it to the world. The charismatic racehorse became a symbol of hope, a beacon of inspiration for those who believed in the transformative power of the sport.

Might and Power's emergence as a star was not just about wins on the track. It was about the connection he forged with a nation. He became more than a racehorse; he became a source of pride, a symbol of Australian excellence. His victories were not just for the stables that trained him or the owners who invested in him; they were for the collective heart of a nation.

In the subsequent chapters, we'll delve into the races that defined the emergence of Might and Power as a star. From the electrifying victories that captured the racing world's attention to the moments that solidified his status as a legend in the making, we'll explore the milestones that marked this remarkable journey.

The emergence of Might and Power as a star was a testament to his extraordinary talent, unyielding spirit, and the support of a nation that believed in him. As we continue to unravel the chapters of his story, we'll witness the ascent of a racehorse who not only became a star in the racing world but also a symbol of Australian racing excellence.

The Journey to 'Might'

In the annals of horse racing, few stories are as captivating as the transformation of a horse from an ordinary competitor to a racing legend. The journey of Might and Power from a promising racehorse to a sensation known as 'Might' represents one of the most remarkable chapters in the history of the sport.

The shift from promising talent to established greatness is often marked by significant milestones. For Might and Power, the turning point came with a newfound determination and a series of remarkable victories. As his reputation continued to grow, the racing world witnessed the emergence of a force that defied all expectations.

The first milestone on the journey to 'Might' was the 1997 Caulfield Cup. It was a race that not only demonstrated his speed and ability but also the character of a racehorse who relished in the heat of competition. His victory in the Caulfield Cup was not just a win; it was a statement that echoed through the racing world.

From the Caulfield Cup, he went on to achieve an astounding victory in the Cox Plate. The 1997 Cox Plate was a race for the ages, one that pitted Might and Power against a field of remarkable competitors. His victory in this prestigious race solidified his status as a horse of immense talent and potential.

But it was the 1997 Melbourne Cup that truly elevated Might and Power to legendary status. The Melbourne Cup is the race that stops a nation, a contest that captures the hearts and hopes of an entire country. His triumphant victory in this iconic race made him more than just a star; it made him an Australian legend.

The journey to 'Might' was not just about winning races; it was about redefining the limits of what a racehorse could achieve. It was about showcasing a level of speed, endurance, and determination that left the racing world in awe. It was about capturing the spirit of a nation and becoming a symbol of Australian excellence.

In this chapter, we'll explore the pivotal moments on the journey to 'Might.' From the Caulfield Cup to the Cox Plate and the Melbourne Cup, we'll relive the races and the victories that marked this extraordinary transformation. We'll witness how a promising racehorse became a sensation, how 'Might' was born from talent, determination, and sheer will.

The journey to 'Might' was a testament to the remarkable talent of this racehorse, the dedication of his trainers and handlers, and the unwavering support of racing enthusiasts across Australia. As we continue to unravel the chapters of his story, we'll discover how 'Might' became more than a name; it became a symbol of the power of racing to transcend the ordinary and achieve the extraordinary.

Chapter 3: Thunder Down Under: The Mighty Saga of Might and Power

The Rise to Fame

The journey of Might and Power was not just a story of remarkable victories; it was a saga that captured the imagination of a nation. It was a journey from promise to prominence, a rise to fame that marked him as one of the most celebrated figures in Australian racing history.

The ascent of Might and Power to fame was not a sudden occurrence; it was the culmination of a series of victories and moments that had the racing world buzzing with anticipation. As he continued to compete and dominate on the track, his reputation grew exponentially, and he transitioned from a talented racehorse to a genuine sensation.

One of the pivotal moments in his rise to fame was the Cox Plate in 1997. This prestigious race, held at Moonee Valley, pitted Might and Power against a field of formidable competitors. It was in this race that he showcased his extraordinary talent and determination, surging ahead to win in a manner that left spectators in awe. The Cox Plate victory was a proclamation that a new star had emerged in Australian racing.

The Caulfield Cup, Melbourne Cup, and Cox Plate victories combined to form the Triple Crown, an achievement that is etched in racing history. Winning these three iconic races in the same season is a rare feat, and Might and Power's accomplishment catapulted him into the realm of racing legends.

As the Triple Crown winner, Might and Power became a symbol of hope and inspiration for racing enthusiasts across the nation. He was more than just a racehorse; he was a phenomenon, a force of nature that embodied the spirit of Australian racing. His fame transcended the sport, reaching into the hearts of those who believed in the magic of the racetrack.

With each victory, his fame continued to grow. He was no longer just a horse known to racing aficionados; he was a household name. The media covered his every move, and the public awaited his races with bated breath. His presence at the track became an event in itself, drawing crowds and cheers that reverberated through the grandstands.

The rise to fame of Might and Power was not just about winning races; it was about capturing the spirit of a nation and providing a source of pride during a time when Australia's racing prowess was in the global spotlight. He became a symbol of excellence, a testament to what could be achieved through talent, dedication, and an unyielding spirit.

In the subsequent chapters, we'll explore the races, the victories, and the moments that contributed to the rise of Might and Power as a national icon. From the thrilling wins to the heartfelt adoration of racing enthusiasts, we'll delve into the milestones that marked this extraordinary journey.

The rise to fame of Might and Power was not just about the horse; it was about the people who believed in him, the trainers and jockeys who guided him, and the spectators who cheered him on. As we continue to unravel the chapters of his story, we'll witness how his fame became a testament to the power of racing to unite a nation and create enduring legends.

The Buzz in the Racing World

In the world of horse racing, there are moments that transcend the ordinary, moments that capture the collective imagination of the racing world. The rise of Might and Power was one such moment, a phenomenon that generated a buzz in the racing world unlike any other.

As Might and Power continued to achieve remarkable victories and accumulate accolades, the racing world was abuzz with anticipation. His electrifying performances had left an indelible mark, and the prospect of witnessing him in action was enough to draw crowds to the racetracks.

One of the pivotal races that contributed to the buzz was the 1997 Caulfield Cup. The manner in which he won, surging ahead with astonishing speed, created a sensation. The racing world took notice, and the anticipation of his upcoming races became a topic of discussion among racing enthusiasts and experts alike.

As he triumphed in the Cox Plate, defeating a field of esteemed competitors, the buzz surrounding Might and Power reached a fever pitch. The Cox Plate is known as the "Race Where Legends Are Made," and his victory in this prestigious contest solidified his status as a legend in the making.

The buzz in the racing world was not limited to the tracks; it extended to the media and the public at large. Newspapers and television broadcasts were filled with stories about the rising star, and the public's interest in his races became a national event. His victories were not just wins; they were celebrations that resonated with racing enthusiasts across the country.

The anticipation reached its pinnacle during the 1997 Melbourne Cup. As the nation's horse, Might and Power carried the hopes and dreams of a country that had fallen in love with him. The Melbourne Cup was not just a race; it was an event that captured the heart of a nation. The buzz leading up to the race was nothing short of electrifying.

On Melbourne Cup day, the entire country tuned in to watch Might and Power in action. The excitement was palpable, and the racing world held its breath as he surged ahead to claim victory. His triumph in the Melbourne Cup was not just a win; it was a moment that brought tears of joy to the eyes of those who believed in the power of racing.

In the chapters that follow, we'll delve into the races and moments that generated the buzz in the racing world. From the Caulfield Cup to the Cox Plate and the Melbourne Cup, we'll explore the victories and the excitement that marked this extraordinary journey.

The buzz in the racing world was not just about the horse; it was about the collective spirit of racing enthusiasts who had found a hero in Might and Power. It was a reminder that horse racing had the power to unite a nation, to capture the imagination, and to create moments that would be cherished for generations to come.

Capturing Hearts and Headlines

In the world of sports, there are moments when an athlete transcends the boundaries of their arena and becomes a cultural icon. Might and Power accomplished just that in the realm of horse racing. His journey from a promising racehorse to a sensation known as 'Might' not only captured the hearts of racing enthusiasts but also dominated headlines in Australia and beyond.

As Might and Power continued to accumulate victories and accolades, he achieved a unique status in Australian racing. He wasn't just a racehorse; he was a symbol of national pride. His charisma, determination, and extraordinary talent resonated with the public, making him a beloved figure across the country.

His captivating early races and subsequent triumphs at iconic events like the Caulfield Cup, the Cox Plate, and the Melbourne Cup turned him into a sensation. Each victory was celebrated not just by those who had a direct stake in his success but by an entire nation that had found a hero in him.

Might and Power's ability to capture hearts was not limited to the racing world. It extended to the broader public who had been introduced to the magic of horse racing through his remarkable journey. The Melbourne Cup, in particular, is known as the "Race That Stops a Nation," and his victory in this prestigious race stopped the nation's heart, if only for a moment, as millions watched in awe.

His triumph in the Melbourne Cup was not just a victory; it was a symbol of hope, determination, and the power of dreams. The headlines that followed his victory were a testament to his significance, not just in the world of sports but in the collective psyche of a nation.

Media outlets across Australia and beyond couldn't get enough of Might and Power. Newspapers featured his victories prominently on their front pages, and television broadcasts dissected his performances. The racing world had a new superstar, and his journey had become a source of inspiration.

The public's love for Might and Power extended beyond the racetrack. He wasn't just a winner; he was a symbol of what could be achieved through dedication, resilience, and a never-give-up attitude. His story was one that resonated with people from all walks of life.

In the subsequent chapters, we'll explore the races and moments that captured hearts and headlines. From his early victories to his triumphs in the Triple Crown races, we'll delve into the milestones that marked this extraordinary journey.

Might and Power's ability to capture hearts and headlines wasn't just about his victories; it was about the indomitable spirit that he represented. He was a reminder that in the world of sports, and in life, the most compelling stories are often those of triumph against the odds. His journey was a reminder that legends are not born; they are made through hard work, perseverance, and the unwavering belief in the power of a dream.

An Era Defined

In the annals of Australian horse racing, there are moments that transcend time, events that define an era and create a legacy that lives on for generations. The era of Might and Power was one such epoch, a period that will forever be etched in the history of Australian racing.

The rise of Might and Power in the late 1990s signaled the beginning of a new era in Australian racing. It was a time when a single racehorse captured the hearts and imagination of a nation, bringing horse racing to the forefront of the Australian sporting landscape. His story became a source of inspiration, a symbol of Australian excellence, and a testament to the enduring spirit of the sport.

The era was marked by a string of historic victories, starting with his electrifying win in the 1997 Caulfield Cup. It was a performance that left spectators in awe, as Might and Power surged ahead with a breathtaking display of speed and power. The victory was more than just a win; it was the opening chapter of an extraordinary saga.

As the racing world witnessed his triumphs in the Cox Plate and the Melbourne Cup, it became clear that a new legend was in the making. The Cox Plate, known as the "Race Where Legends Are Made," saw Might and Power defeat a field of formidable competitors. His Melbourne Cup victory was a moment of pure magic, as he carried the hopes of a nation to a historic win.

The era of Might and Power was not just about winning races; it was about the collective spirit of a nation that rallied behind a horse they considered their own. He was more than a racehorse; he was a symbol of hope and inspiration during a time when Australia's racing prowess was on the global stage.

The media covered his every move, and his races became national events. Newspaper headlines were dominated by his victories, and television broadcasts dissected his performances. He was not just a star in the racing world; he was a cultural icon who transcended the boundaries of the sport.

The era was defined by the unwavering support of racing enthusiasts who cheered him on at every race. It was marked by the jubilation of those who had witnessed his triumphs and the tears of joy that flowed when he crossed the finish line in first place. Might and Power had become more than a horse; he was a symbol of the power of dreams.

In the chapters that follow, we'll delve deeper into the era defined by Might and Power. We'll explore the races, the victories, and the emotions that marked this extraordinary period. From the adoration of fans to the impact on

Australian racing, we'll witness how this era left an indelible mark on the sport and the nation.

The era of Might and Power was a reminder that in the world of sports, there are moments that stand the test of time. It was an epoch defined by the spirit of a champion, the support of a nation, and the belief that dreams can become reality. The legacy of this era endures, a testament to the power of horse racing to create enduring legends.

Chapter 4: From Birth to Glory: The Might and Power Chronicle

The Development of Might

Greatness is not simply bestowed upon an individual; it is forged through a combination of innate talent, relentless effort, and careful nurturing. The journey of Might and Power from his early days to the pinnacle of Australian racing was a testament to the development of a racehorse who would become a legend.

Might and Power was born in New Zealand on October 19, 1993, a son of the sire Zabeel and dam Benediction. From the outset, he carried a pedigree that hinted at his potential. His lineage was impressive, with Zabeel being a renowned stallion known for producing exceptional racehorses.

The development of Might and Power began in the hands of his breeders and early trainers. His early years were marked by the careful guidance of those who recognized his raw talent. The foundation of his success lay in the nurturing of his natural abilities.

It was evident early on that Might and Power possessed qualities that set him apart from his peers. His athleticism, strength, and a relentless desire to compete were clear indicators of a future champion in the making. As he took his first steps on the training tracks, it became apparent that he had the potential to achieve something extraordinary.

One of the pivotal moments in his development came when he was introduced to legendary trainer John Wheeler. Wheeler recognized the latent talent in the young colt and took on the responsibility of honing his skills. Under Wheeler's guidance, Might and Power underwent a transformation that would define his career.

Wheeler's training methods, coupled with the dedication of the stable staff, played a crucial role in shaping Might and Power into a champion. The training regimen was rigorous, emphasizing not only physical conditioning but also mental fortitude. Might and Power was molded into a racehorse capable of conquering the toughest of challenges.

His early races provided the platform for his development. Each competition was a lesson, a step towards maturity. As he tasted victory and faced adversity, he grew in experience and confidence. It was in these early races that the world began to glimpse the potential of 'Might,' and his development gathered momentum.

The road to glory was marked by a series of milestones. As he continued to train, compete, and evolve, it became clear that he was destined for greatness. The development of Might and Power was a journey of growth, learning, and the relentless pursuit of excellence.

In the subsequent chapters, we'll explore the stages of his development in detail. From his early years to his transformation under John Wheeler's guidance, we'll delve into the moments that shaped the young colt into a racehorse of extraordinary potential.

The development of Might and Power was not just about physical attributes; it was about the spirit that burned within him. It was about the belief in his own potential and the unwavering commitment of those who saw something special in him. As we continue to unravel the chapters of his story, we'll witness how this development laid the foundation for the legend he would become.

Setting the Stage for Glory

In the world of horse racing, success is not just about raw talent; it's about the meticulous preparation, strategic decisions, and unwavering dedication that pave the way for a horse to achieve greatness. For Might and Power, the journey from an unassuming foal to a racing legend was marked by a series of strategic decisions and careful planning that set the stage for his remarkable career.

As he continued to develop under the watchful eye of trainer John Wheeler, the stage was being set for Might and Power to make a lasting mark on the Australian racing scene. Wheeler's training methods emphasized both physical and mental conditioning, preparing the young colt for the challenges that lay ahead. It was a process that instilled in Might and Power the resilience and strength needed to overcome adversity.

One of the pivotal decisions made during this stage of his development was the transition from New Zealand to Australia. While New Zealand had played a crucial role in nurturing his early years, the move to Australia would prove to be a turning point in his career. It was a strategic decision that would expose him to a more competitive racing environment and set the stage for greater challenges.

Might and Power's first taste of Australian racing came in 1996, and it was a moment that would foreshadow his future glory. He made his Australian debut at Rosehill Gardens, and his performance left a strong impression. The Australian racing community was beginning to take notice of this rising star, and the stage was being prepared for his ascent.

His early races in Australia were stepping stones, each one designed to prepare him for the challenges of the elite racing circuit. He began to accumulate victories, showcasing not only his speed but also his ability to handle different race conditions. The development of his racing skills was a deliberate process, with each race contributing to his growth as a racehorse.

Another critical aspect of setting the stage for Might and Power's glory was the selection of jockeys. Jockey Jim Cassidy played a pivotal role in his career, forming a formidable partnership that would lead to numerous victories. Cassidy's understanding of the horse's abilities and his ability to bring out the best in Might and Power became a defining factor in the horse's success.

The stage was also set through strategic race selections. The decision to enter him in the Caulfield Cup, a race known for its competitiveness and prestige, was a bold move that would define his career. His victory in this iconic race was a statement of intent, signaling that he was a force to be reckoned with on the Australian racing scene.

In the chapters that follow, we'll delve deeper into the strategic decisions, race selections, and moments that set the stage for Might and Power's glory. From the move to Australia to the partnerships that shaped his career, we'll explore the deliberate choices that contributed to his remarkable journey.

Setting the stage for glory was not just about winning races; it was about the careful planning, the foresight of his trainers and owners, and the vision of those who believed in his potential. As we continue to unravel the chapters of his story, we'll witness how this stage-setting process would lead to an era of unprecedented success and a legacy that endures to this day.

Unprecedented Achievements

In the realm of horse racing, the word 'legendary' is often used to describe exceptional horses. Yet, there are a rare few whose achievements transcend this label, and Might and Power was undeniably one of them. His journey from an unassuming foal to a racing sensation was marked by a string of unprecedented achievements that elevated him to the status of an Australian racing icon.

One of the defining moments of Might and Power's career was his historic victory in the 1997 Caulfield Cup. This race, known for its competitiveness and prestige, was where he announced himself as a force to be reckoned with. What made this victory truly exceptional was the manner in which he achieved it. Might and Power not only won the race but did so in record-breaking fashion. His performance left spectators in awe as he surged ahead with astonishing speed and strength. The Caulfield Cup became a stage for unprecedented achievement.

As he continued to conquer major races, the records began to fall like dominoes. Might and Power's remarkable feats included record wins in the Yalumba Stakes, the Victoria Derby, and the Cox Plate. Each victory was not just a win but a record-breaking, history-making event. The horse's name began to feature prominently in the record books of Australian racing.

Perhaps the most celebrated of his unprecedented achievements was his victory in the 1997 Melbourne Cup. The Melbourne Cup is Australia's most prestigious and iconic race, often referred to as the "Race That Stops a Nation." In the lead-up to the event, the anticipation was palpable, and the expectations were sky-high. Might and Power not only met those expectations but exceeded them. His victory in the Melbourne Cup was not just a race win; it was a moment that etched his name in the annals of Australian sporting history.

The Melbourne Cup win marked several firsts. He became the first horse in 53 years to win both the Caulfield Cup and the Melbourne Cup in the same year. He set a new weight-carrying record for a four-year-old in the Melbourne Cup, an achievement that underlined his exceptional ability.

Beyond the records and victories, it was the manner in which Might and Power achieved these feats that captured the imagination of the racing world. He wasn't just winning races; he was doing so with style and grace. His powerful surges to the finish line, his ability to carry weight, and his sheer determination set him apart.

The unprecedented achievements of Might and Power were not just about the numbers; they were about the spirit of a champion. He had become a symbol of excellence, a testament to what could be achieved through dedication and unwavering belief. His story was one of inspiration, proving that the extraordinary is possible when one dares to dream.

In the chapters that follow, we'll delve deeper into these unprecedented achievements. From the records to the historic wins, we'll explore how Might and Power left an indelible mark on Australian racing, rewriting the record books and creating moments that continue to be celebrated.

Might and Power's achievements were not just about the horse; they were about the collective spirit of racing enthusiasts who had found a hero in him. It was a reminder that in the world of sports, the most compelling stories are often those of triumph against the odds. His journey was a testament that legends are not born; they are made through hard work, perseverance, and the unwavering belief in the power of a dream.

Racing's Prodigy

In the world of horse racing, certain individuals stand out as prodigies—those with a natural gift, an innate talent that sets them apart from their peers. Might and Power was unquestionably one of these prodigies, a horse whose prowess on the track left spectators and experts alike in awe.

From his earliest days, Might and Power displayed signs of prodigious ability. Born in New Zealand on October 19, 1993, he carried a lineage of excellence, with his sire Zabeel being renowned for producing exceptional racehorses. His pedigree hinted at the potential within him, and it didn't take long for those around him to realize that they were in the presence of a racing prodigy.

One of the characteristics that defined Might and Power as a prodigy was his innate athleticism. His physical attributes, including his impressive speed and raw strength, were evident from a young age. He possessed a grace and agility that set him apart. As he took his first steps on the training tracks, it became increasingly clear that this colt was not ordinary—he was a racing prodigy in the making.

As he began to compete in his early races, it was evident that Might and Power possessed a racing instinct that few could match. He seemed to understand the dynamics of a race, pacing himself and making strategic moves that belied his age. His racing intelligence set him apart as a prodigy who could read the track and his competitors with uncanny precision.

His early races, which included victories at Rosehill Gardens and Canterbury Park, were showcases of his prodigious ability. He didn't just win races; he dominated them, often finishing well ahead of his competitors. His performances were characterized by bursts of speed and an ability to surge past rivals with breathtaking ease. The racing world was taking notice of this exceptional prodigy.

Yet, being a prodigy was not just about winning races; it was about doing so with a unique flair and charisma. Might and Power possessed a showmanship that endeared him to racing enthusiasts. His races were not just events; they were experiences, filled with moments of awe and excitement. He was not just a racehorse; he was a performer, and the track was his stage.

As he continued to develop and compete, the label of 'prodigy' stuck with him. He was a colt who had not only met but exceeded expectations. His performances were no longer surprising; they were expected. Might and Power had become the face of Australian racing, a prodigy who had captured the hearts of the nation.

The Melbourne Cup victory in 1997 was the crowning moment of his prodigious career. It was a race where his prodigious talent met the grandest stage in Australian racing. The nation watched in awe as this racing prodigy carried the weight of expectations and history on his shoulders and emerged victorious.

In the chapters that follow, we'll explore the moments that defined Might and Power as a racing prodigy. From his early years to his transformation under trainer John Wheeler's guidance, we'll delve into the extraordinary talent that set him apart. His journey was not just about winning races; it was about the charisma, the showmanship, and the prodigious ability that captured the imagination of all who witnessed it.

Might and Power's status as a racing prodigy wasn't just about his physical prowess; it was about the spirit of a champion. It was a reminder that in the world of sports, the most exceptional talents are those who combine their innate gifts with unwavering dedication and the unshakable belief in their own potential. His journey was a testament that legends are not born; they are made through hard work, perseverance, and the unwavering belief in the power of a dream.

Chapter 5: Unstoppable Force: The Triumphs of Might and Power

Dominating the Competition

In the world of horse racing, there are horses, and then there are champions. Might and Power firmly belonged to the latter category, and his journey in the chapter titled "Unstoppable Force: The Triumphs of Might and Power" is a testament to his dominance and excellence on the racetrack.

As he progressed through his racing career, it became abundantly clear that Might and Power was a force to be reckoned with. His innate talent and relentless training had transformed him into a racehorse of unparalleled skill and ability. He was not merely competing; he was dominating the competition.

One of the defining characteristics of his racing style was his explosive speed. When Might and Power surged forward, it was as if he possessed an extra gear that left his competitors in the dust. His breathtaking bursts of acceleration were unmatched, and he used them strategically to outpace his rivals.

His dominance was evident in the races he entered, where he often finished with significant leads. He wasn't content with just winning; he aimed to win decisively. His victories were not by mere lengths; they were often by margins that left spectators in awe.

An example of his dominance was his performance in the Yalumba Stakes, a race where he set a new weight-carrying record. Carrying a substantial weight, Might and Power not only won but did so with remarkable ease. The victory was not just a win; it was a statement of his supremacy over the competition.

As he continued to conquer major races, including the Victoria Derby and the Cox Plate, he was not just competing; he was showcasing his unparalleled talent. The Cox Plate, known as the "Race Where Legends Are Made," was where he faced formidable competitors, including some of the best in the world. His victory in this race was a display of dominance that etched his name in the annals of racing history.

Yet, what truly cemented his reputation as a dominant force was his victory in the Melbourne Cup. This race, often referred to as the "Race That Stops a Nation," was where the eyes of the world were fixed. The weight he carried, the competition he faced, and the expectations he shouldered were immense. And yet, Might and Power rose above it all to claim victory, once again showcasing his dominance.

His domination extended beyond just the win-loss column. It was in the manner in which he raced, the confidence with which he approached each competition, and the fear he struck into the hearts of his rivals. He was not just a competitor; he was a psychological force, and his presence alone was often enough to unsettle the competition.

In the chapters that follow, we'll delve deeper into his dominance. From the records he set to the moments of sheer brilliance on the racetrack, we'll explore how Might and Power was more than just a racehorse; he was a symbol of excellence, a reminder that champions are not merely winners but those who redefine the sport.

Might and Power's journey as an unstoppable force was not just about physical prowess; it was about the spirit of a champion. It was a reminder that in the world of sports, true greatness is achieved through a combination of talent, dedication, and the unyielding pursuit of excellence. His story was a testament that legends are not born; they are made through hard work, perseverance, and the unwavering belief in the power of a dream.

Breaking Records

In the realm of sports, records stand as the benchmarks of excellence, achievements that set the standard for generations to come. Might and Power was not just a racehorse; he was a record-breaker, an equine athlete who rewrote the record books and left an indelible mark on Australian horse racing.

One of the records that catapulted Might and Power into the limelight was his performance in the 1997 Caulfield Cup. While winning this prestigious race was a remarkable feat in itself, it was the manner in which he did it that astounded all. He not only won the race but did so while carrying an unprecedented weight, setting a new weight-carrying record for four-year-olds in the Caulfield Cup. It was a record that spoke of his exceptional ability to handle the heaviest of burdens.

But that was just the beginning. In the same year, Might and Power would go on to break more records. His victory in the Victoria Derby was a historic one, as he became the first horse to complete the Caulfield Cup-Victoria Derby double in 49 years. It was a record that highlighted his versatility and ability to excel in different racing conditions.

The Cox Plate, often referred to as the "Race Where Legends Are Made," was another stage where Might and

Power etched his name into the record books. His dominant victory in this race not only added another feather to his cap but also showcased his remarkable speed and endurance. It was a race that witnessed history being made as he set new records.

But it was the Melbourne Cup that would cement his legacy as a record-breaker. As the race that holds the highest significance in Australian horse racing, winning the Melbourne Cup alone is a monumental achievement. However, Might and Power went a step further. He became the first horse in 53 years to win both the Caulfield Cup and the Melbourne Cup in the same year. It was a record that defied the odds and spoke of his extraordinary talent.

His achievements were not just about setting records but also about doing so in grand style. Each of his record-breaking victories was marked by breathtaking surges of speed, extraordinary feats of strength, and the exuberance of a true champion. He didn't just win races; he redefined what was possible in horse racing.

Yet, his record-breaking journey wasn't limited to victories alone. In the Yalumba Stakes, he would once again set a new weight-carrying record, showcasing his ability to carry substantial weights while still dominating the competition. His record-breaking performances transcended individual races; they became a testament to his enduring excellence.

In the chapters that follow, we'll explore the moments that defined Might and Power as a record-breaker. From the weight records to the historic wins, we'll delve into how he left an indelible mark on Australian racing, rewriting the record books and creating moments that continue to be celebrated.

Might and Power's journey as a record-breaker was not just about the numbers; it was about the spirit of a champion. It was a reminder that in the world of sports, the most exceptional talents are those who push the boundaries of what is considered possible. His story was a testament that legends are not born; they are made through hard work, perseverance, and the unwavering belief in the power of a dream.

The Power Within

Great racehorses possess more than just speed and strength; they have an intangible quality that sets them apart. For Might and Power, this quality was the undeniable and awe-inspiring power that resided within him. It wasn't just physical prowess; it was a spirit that burned bright, driving him to achieve the extraordinary.

One of the defining aspects of Might and Power was his astonishing acceleration. When he decided it was time to surge forward, he did so with an explosive burst of speed that left both rivals and spectators in awe. It was a power that seemed to come from within, a reservoir of energy that he tapped into at precisely the right moments.

This power was most evident in the 1997 Caulfield Cup, where he carried an unprecedented weight to victory. The manner in which he not only carried the weight but did so with such ease and grace spoke of the immense reserves of power within him. It was as if he had harnessed the energy of a thunderstorm and channeled it into his race.

In the Victoria Derby, his power was showcased once again. He surged ahead with such force and vigor that it left no doubt about his supremacy. His power was not just about speed but also about the tenacity to maintain his pace and the determination to outclass his rivals. It was the power of a champion.

The Cox Plate was another arena where his power within was evident. In a race known for its competitiveness and grueling nature, Might and Power displayed his extraordinary power by leading from start to finish. It was a performance that left the racing world in admiration of the horse's unyielding determination and inner strength.

But it was the Melbourne Cup where his power shone brightest. The race that carries the weight of history and expectation is often referred to as the "Race That Stops a Nation." It was a race where the power of the moment could be overwhelming. Yet, Might and Power carried not only the weight of expectations but also the literal weight of a record-breaking load. His power, both physical and mental, came to the forefront as he surged ahead in the final stretch, creating a moment that would be etched in Australian racing history.

His power wasn't just about winning races; it was about the unbreakable spirit that drove him to perform at his best. It was about the heart of a champion that refused to be defeated. His power was in the courage to face adversity, the determination to overcome challenges, and the unshakable belief in his own potential.

In the chapters that follow, we'll delve deeper into this power within. From his remarkable performances to the unyielding spirit that defined his career, we'll explore how Might and Power was more than just a racehorse; he was a symbol of excellence, a reminder that champions are not merely those who win but those who carry within them an unquenchable fire.

Might and Power's journey was not just about physical prowess; it was about the spirit of a champion. It was a reminder that in the world of sports, the most compelling stories are often those of triumph against the odds. His journey was a testament that legends are not born; they are made through hard work, perseverance, and the unwavering belief in the power of a dream.

Celebrations of Triumph

In the world of sports, victory is not just about the result; it's about the celebration that follows. Might and Power didn't just win races; he won hearts and ignited celebrations that echoed through time. His triumphs were more than just moments of victory; they were celebrations of excellence, displays of joy and camaraderie that united a nation.

The 1997 Caulfield Cup marked the beginning of a series of exuberant celebrations. As Might and Power crossed the finish line, carrying a weight that had never been carried by a four-year-old before, the crowd erupted into thunderous applause. Spectators in the grandstands and at home watched in awe, recognizing that they were witnessing history in the making. The celebrations that followed were a testament to the horse's indomitable spirit and the joy he brought to racing enthusiasts.

The Victoria Derby was another occasion for celebration. As Might and Power surged to victory, the grandstands reverberated with cheers and applause. It was a moment that embodied the thrill of racing, the exhilaration of watching a champion in action. The celebrations spilled into the streets as fans, trainers, and jockeys joined in commemorating the remarkable achievement.

The Cox Plate, a race often referred to as the "Race Where Legends Are Made," was a stage for jubilant celebrations. As Might and Power led from start to finish, spectators couldn't contain their excitement. The win was not just a victory; it was a triumph of spirit and an ode to racing greatness. The celebrations at Moonee Valley that day were a fitting tribute to the horse's power and prowess.

But it was the Melbourne Cup that set the stage for the grandest celebration of them all. As Might and Power surged ahead in the final stretch, a hush fell over the crowd, followed by a deafening roar of triumph. Spectators, many of whom had come to watch history being made, erupted in jubilation. The nation celebrated the victory of a horse who had carried not just the weight of a nation but the weight of expectations and history.

The celebrations extended far beyond the racetrack. Cities, towns, and communities across Australia joined in the euphoria. Parades were organized, and public events became venues for celebrating the champion. Might and Power became a symbol of pride, a horse who had transcended the sport and entered the realm of national legend.

These celebrations were not just about victory; they were about the collective joy that sport can bring. Might and Power became a unifying force, a horse who had the remarkable ability to bring people together, regardless of their backgrounds or differences. He was a symbol of excellence that the nation rallied around.

In the chapters that follow, we'll explore the enduring impact of these celebrations. From the parades to the accolades, we'll delve into how Might and Power's triumphs were not just moments in time but experiences that continue to be celebrated. His story was more than just winning races; it was about creating memories, inspiring generations, and celebrating the power of a dream.

Might and Power's journey as a cause for celebration was not just about victory; it was about the spirit of a champion. It was a reminder that in the world of sports, the most enduring legacies are often those that bring joy and inspiration to the lives of people. His journey was a testament that legends are not born; they are made through hard work, perseverance, and the unwavering belief in the power of a dream.

Chapter 6: Champion of the Track: The Might and Power Legacy

Australian Horse of the Year

In the annals of Australian horse racing, the title of "Horse of the Year" is the highest honor a racehorse can attain. It's a distinction reserved for the equine athletes who have not only excelled in their performances but have left an indelible mark on the sport. Might and Power achieved this pinnacle of recognition, becoming the Australian Horse of the Year and securing his legacy as one of the greatest in the history of Australian racing.

His journey to this esteemed title was marked by a string of extraordinary victories that captivated the racing world. The Caulfield Cup, the Victoria Derby, the Cox Plate, and the Melbourne Cup were the jewels in his crown, and each win was a testament to his exceptional talent and power.

The Australian Horse of the Year title is not awarded lightly. It requires consistent excellence and a level of performance that sets a horse apart from the competition. For Might and Power, this recognition was not just about a single season of success but a culmination of achievements that spanned his racing career.

His versatility was one of the key factors that set him apart. He was equally at ease on various tracks and distances, showcasing his adaptability and versatility. This broad spectrum of capabilities contributed to his reputation as a true all-rounder in Australian racing.

The recognition as the Australian Horse of the Year was not solely based on statistics; it was also about the impact he had on the sport. His presence drew crowds, and his performances created unforgettable moments in racing history. His victories in prestigious races were not just wins; they were events that defined an era.

The award was not just about the horse; it was also a reflection of the dedication of his trainer, jockey, and the entire team behind him. Their unwavering commitment to bringing out the best in Might and Power was a crucial factor in his journey to becoming a champion.

Receiving the title of Australian Horse of the Year was a moment of celebration not just for the horse's connections but for the entire nation. It was an acknowledgment of the greatness that Australian racing had witnessed and a testament to the fact that champions are not just born; they are made through hard work, dedication, and the relentless pursuit of excellence.

In the chapters that follow, we'll delve deeper into the legacy of Might and Power. We'll explore how his recognition as the Australian Horse of the Year was not just an accolade but a reflection of the enduring impact he had on Australian racing. His story is a reminder that legends are not just those who win races; they are those who inspire a nation and leave an indelible mark on the sport they love.

Might and Power's journey as the Australian Horse of the Year was not just about titles and accolades; it was about the spirit of a champion. It was a reminder that in the world of sports, true greatness is achieved through a combination of talent, dedication, and the unyielding pursuit of excellence. His story was a testament that legends are not born; they are made through hard work, perseverance, and the unwavering belief in the power of a dream.

The Spirit of a Champion

In the world of sports, the term "champion" extends beyond the mere act of winning. It encompasses qualities that go beyond the physical realm—qualities that define the spirit of a true champion. Might and Power, the Australian legend, embodied the essence of what it means to be a champion.

His spirit was a unique blend of determination, courage, and resilience. It was a spirit that drove him to overcome adversity and achieve greatness. It was a spirit that endeared him to fans and solidified his place in the annals of Australian racing history.

Might and Power's journey to greatness wasn't without its challenges. His early years were marked by setbacks and uncertainties. Yet, it was during these formative years that the seeds of his champion spirit were sown. He displayed a determination that was unshakable, a drive to prove himself even when the odds were stacked against him.

As he embarked on his racing career, it was evident that he possessed a champion's heart. He had the will to win, a spirit that refused to accept anything less than the best. It was a spirit that drove him to not just compete but to dominate his rivals.

His record-breaking victory in the 1997 Caulfield Cup was a testament to his champion spirit. Carrying a weight that no four-year-old had ever carried before, he defied conventional wisdom and surged to victory. It wasn't just about the win; it was about the courage to take on a challenge that others deemed impossible.

The Melbourne Cup, often referred to as the "Race That Stops a Nation," was another stage where his spirit shone. The weight of history and expectations bore down on him, but he didn't falter. Instead, he displayed a champion's mentality, surging ahead in the final stretch to secure victory. His spirit was a beacon of hope for those who believed in the power of dreams.

The essence of a champion isn't just about victory; it's also about the impact one leaves on the sport. Might and Power's spirit was so infectious that it united a nation. He became a symbol of hope and inspiration, proof that with unwavering determination, even the loftiest goals could be achieved.

His spirit extended beyond the racetrack. It was about his interactions with fans, his bond with his jockey, and the way he captured the hearts of those who followed his journey. He wasn't just a horse; he was a living embodiment of the spirit of a champion.

In the chapters that follow, we'll delve deeper into this champion spirit. From his early years to his triumphant moments, we'll explore how Might and Power was more than just a racehorse; he was a symbol of excellence, a reminder that champions are not merely those who win but those who carry within them an unquenchable fire.

Might and Power's journey as a champion was not just about victories; it was about the spirit of a true champion. It was a reminder that in the world of sports, the most compelling stories are often those of triumph against the odds. His journey was a testament that legends are not born; they are made through hard work, perseverance, and the unwavering belief in the power of a dream.

The Fan's Favorite

In the world of sports, fans play a pivotal role in creating the atmosphere that defines an event. They bring passion, enthusiasm, and an unwavering loyalty to their favorite athletes. For Might and Power, this support wasn't just a testament to his prowess on the racetrack; it was a reflection of the deep connection he forged with racing enthusiasts, making him the fan's favorite.

Might and Power wasn't just a racehorse; he was an icon. His performances on the track created moments that were etched in the hearts of fans. His spirit of determination and resilience resonated with those who admired the underdog rising to greatness. He was the embodiment of the champion that fans rallied behind.

One of the key factors that made Might and Power the fan's favorite was his approachability. Unlike some racing superstars who remained aloof, he had a charm that endeared him to all. He was approachable, both in demeanor and in accessibility. Fans could witness his training sessions, interact with his trainers and jockey, and even meet him up close. This sense of connection created a bond that went beyond the racetrack.

His racing style was another factor that drew fans. He was known for his electrifying bursts of speed and his knack for staging come-from-behind victories. Fans loved the suspense and excitement that his races brought. They cheered for him not just because he won but because his races were exhilarating journeys, filled with unexpected twists and turns.

The 1997 Caulfield Cup, where he carried an unprecedented weight to victory, was a prime example of how he won the hearts of fans. His triumph against the odds was a tale of underdog victory that resonated with those who believed in the power of perseverance. Fans at the racecourse and those watching at home were caught in the thrall of his historic win.

The Melbourne Cup was another instance where he became the people's champion. In a race that carried the weight of history and expectation, he powered ahead in the final stretch, securing victory and etching his name in Australian racing folklore. The roar of the crowd was a testament to the fanfare he generated.

But it wasn't just about winning the big races; it was about the impact he had on those who followed him. He became a horse for the people, an athlete who transcended the boundaries of the sport. He had a charisma that extended beyond the racetrack, capturing the imaginations of fans across generations.

In the chapters that follow, we'll delve deeper into his status as the fan's favorite. From the parades and public events that celebrated his victories to the personal stories of fans who were touched by his journey, we'll explore how Might and Power was not just a racehorse but a symbol of hope and inspiration.

Might and Power's journey as the fan's favorite was not just about winning races; it was about the spirit of a champion that touched the lives of many. It was a reminder that in the world of sports, the most enduring legacies are often those that bring joy and inspiration to the lives of people. His story was a testament that legends are not born; they are made through hard work, perseverance, and the unwavering belief in the power of a dream.

Beyond the Racetrack

While the racetrack was the stage where Might and Power dazzled the world with his performances, his impact extended far beyond the confines of the turf. His legacy, like that of true champions, transcended the boundaries of his sport, leaving an indelible mark on various aspects of Australian life.

One of the remarkable ways Might and Power extended his influence was through his charity work. He became an ambassador for various causes, using his fame and recognition to raise funds and awareness. His involvement in charitable activities was a reflection of the champion spirit that resided in him. Whether it was supporting children's hospitals or contributing to causes for animal welfare, he used his stature for the betterment of society.

His connection with fans continued outside the racetrack. He often participated in public events, where admirers could meet him up close. These interactions were more than just photo opportunities; they were moments that fans cherished. For many, meeting Might and Power was a dream come true, a memory they held dear.

Might and Power's impact on the racing industry was profound. He inspired generations of jockeys, trainers, and breeders. His journey from an underdog to a champion served as a testament to the limitless possibilities in the sport. He changed the way people viewed racing and instilled a sense of pride in Australian racing.

His influence extended to the breeding industry as well. His success on the track led to a surge in interest in his bloodline. He became a sire, producing a lineage of potential champions who carried his legacy forward. His offspring proved that greatness could be passed on, and his name continued to grace the winners' circles.

In the chapters that follow, we'll delve deeper into the enduring impact of Might and Power beyond the racetrack. From his charity work to his role in inspiring future champions, we'll explore how he was more than just a racehorse; he was a symbol of hope and a catalyst for change.

Might and Power's journey beyond the racetrack was not just about records and titles; it was about the spirit of a champion that touched the lives of many. It was a reminder that in the world of sports, true greatness is achieved not only through victories but through the ability to inspire, to create change, and to leave an indelible mark on the hearts of people. His story was a testament that legends are not born; they are made through hard work, perseverance, and the unwavering belief in the power of a dream.

Chapter 7: Caulfield to Cup: The Mighty Rise of Might and Power

The Caulfield Cup Triumph

In the annals of Australian horse racing, there are victories, and then there are historic triumphs that etch a horse's name in gold. Might and Power's victory in the 1997 Caulfield Cup was unquestionably one of the latter—a moment that transcended racing and became a defining chapter in the history of the sport.

The Caulfield Cup, often dubbed as "the world's richest 2400-meter handicap," was already a prestigious race by the time Might and Power entered the scene. It attracted a field of top-class stayers from across the globe, and victory was a coveted prize for any horse. But in 1997, the Caulfield Cup took on a new significance, thanks to an unassuming bay gelding with a white blaze on his forehead.

For Might and Power, the road to the Caulfield Cup was one marked with potential and promise. His early years were spent in the shadows, a promising young horse with the potential to surprise the racing world. Under the guidance of his trainer, Jack Denham, and the partnership with jockey Jim Cassidy, he underwent rigorous training to prepare for the challenges that lay ahead.

The stage was set for a showdown of epic proportions. On a sunny Melbourne afternoon in October 1997, Might and Power entered the Caulfield racecourse with a weight on his back that had never been seen before. Carrying 58 kilograms, a weight that was often considered insurmountable for a four-year-old, he was poised for a test of not only his physical capabilities but his spirit and determination.

As the field thundered down the final stretch, Might and Power found himself surrounded by formidable competitors. The pressure was intense, and the weight was an ever-present reminder of the enormity of the task. But he dug deep, finding an inner reserve of power that defied expectations. In a breathtaking display of strength and stamina, he surged ahead to clinch victory.

The roar of the crowd was deafening, a testament to the awe-inspiring feat they had witnessed. Might and Power had not only won the Caulfield Cup; he had done it in record-breaking fashion. His time of 2 minutes and 25.29 seconds stood as a record that remained unbroken for years.

The victory in the Caulfield Cup was more than just a win; it was a symbol of the power of determination and the triumph of the underdog. It was a moment that united a nation in celebration, as Australians reveled in the success of their new hero.

In the chapters that follow, we'll delve deeper into this historic moment in Australian racing history. We'll explore the preparations, the race itself, and the aftermath that solidified Might and Power's place as a true legend. The Caulfield Cup was a pivotal moment, and it set the stage for what would become an extraordinary racing career.

Might and Power's victory in the Caulfield Cup was not just about records and titles; it was about the spirit of a champion that defied expectations and showcased the power of resilience. It was a reminder that in the world of sports, true greatness is achieved through a combination of talent, dedication, and the unyielding pursuit of excellence. His story was a testament that legends are not born; they are made through hard work, perseverance, and the unwavering belief in the power of a dream.

Road to Melbourne

As the sun set on the Caulfield Cup, and Might and Power basked in the glory of an historic victory, Australian racing had a new sensation. The four-year-old bay gelding with a white blaze had defied expectations, carrying an unprecedented weight to triumph. But this was only the beginning of his remarkable journey.

After the euphoria of the Caulfield Cup settled, the racing world turned its gaze toward the next grand challenge—the Melbourne Cup. Often referred to as "the Race That Stops a Nation," the Melbourne Cup was not just a prestigious race; it was a cultural phenomenon, a moment when the entire country held its breath, waiting for history to be made.

Might and Power's success at Caulfield had ignited the hopes and dreams of racing enthusiasts across Australia. It was now Melbourne's turn to witness the might and power of the horse who had captured the nation's heart. His journey to Flemington, the hallowed grounds of the Melbourne Cup, was a path laden with anticipation, challenges, and an ever-mounting weight of expectations.

The road to Melbourne was more than just a physical journey; it was a psychological odyssey. The weight of history and the weight of the handicaps combined to create an atmosphere of immense pressure. Racing experts and pundits wondered whether Might and Power could repeat the magic he had displayed at Caulfield.

But amidst all the speculation, there was a quiet confidence in the Might and Power camp. Trainer Jack Denham, jockey Jim Cassidy, and the entire team knew they had a champion in their midst. They believed in the horse's spirit, his indomitable will to win, and his capacity to rise to the occasion.

The buildup to the Melbourne Cup was a blend of anticipation and preparation. Training sessions were meticulous, and every aspect of Might and Power's well-being was taken into account. His diet, fitness, and mental state were all closely monitored, ensuring that he would be at his absolute best when the moment arrived.

As the first Tuesday in November drew near, the city of Melbourne buzzed with excitement. Flemington Racecourse underwent a transformation, with the grandstands and gardens adorned with an array of colors. The Melbourne Cup Carnival had begun, and the eyes of the nation were focused on the main event.

Might and Power's arrival at Flemington was a moment of jubilation. He was welcomed by adoring fans, well-wishers, and curious onlookers. The weight of expectation was immense, but it only seemed to fuel his determination. His calm demeanor and the sparkle in his eyes were a testament to the champion within.

In the chapters that follow, we'll explore the electrifying atmosphere of Melbourne in the lead-up to the Melbourne Cup. We'll delve into the challenges faced and the unwavering belief that carried Might and Power through the journey. The road to Melbourne was not just a physical voyage; it was a test of character and an exploration of the horse's heart.

Might and Power's journey to the Melbourne Cup was more than just a race; it was a pilgrimage that showcased the power of belief, the weight of expectations, and the unyielding spirit of a champion. It was a reminder that in the world of sports, the most enduring legends are often those who can handle the pressure and rise above the fray. His story was a testament that legends are not born; they are made through hard work, perseverance, and the unwavering belief in the power of a dream.

November 1997: A Historic Day

The first Tuesday in November is a date etched in the hearts of Australians, a day when the nation's attention turns to Flemington Racecourse for the running of the Melbourne Cup. In 1997, this iconic event held even greater significance, thanks to the presence of a horse who had captured the imagination of a country. That horse was Might and Power, and November 4, 1997, would become a historic day in Australian racing history.

As the Melbourne Cup Carnival reached its pinnacle, Flemington was a tapestry of colors, emotions, and anticipation. The atmosphere was electric, with fans, punters, and racing enthusiasts converging to witness a spectacle that extended beyond the racetrack. It was a celebration of culture, fashion, and, above all, the power of sport to unite a nation.

For Might and Power, this was the moment that would define his legacy. The Caulfield Cup victory had hinted at his extraordinary potential, but the Melbourne Cup was the true test of a champion. Could he overcome not only a formidable field of competitors but also the weight of expectations?

The buildup to the Melbourne Cup was a crescendo of excitement. Might and Power's preparation had been meticulous, and he had demonstrated his form in lead-up races. Trainer Jack Denham and jockey Jim Cassidy were well aware of the horse's capabilities, and they approached the race with a quiet confidence.

As the horses paraded in the mounting yard, the tension was palpable. The eyes of the nation were on Might and Power, and his every move was scrutinized. The weight of history loomed, as no horse had carried 56 kilograms to victory since the legendary Phar Lap in 1930.

The starting gates opened, and the thundering hooves of the field echoed through Flemington. Might and Power settled into the race, biding his time, and waiting for the perfect moment. As the horses turned into the final straight, he made his move, surging ahead with a burst of speed that left his competitors struggling in his wake.

The roar of the crowd was deafening as Might and Power crossed the finish line, securing victory in the Melbourne Cup. History had been made, as he became only the fifth horse in history to win the Caulfield Cup and Melbourne Cup double in the same year.

The nation erupted in celebration. Australians from all walks of life rejoiced in the victory of a horse who had carried their hopes and dreams to the ultimate triumph.

Might and Power had not only won a race; he had won the hearts of a nation.

In the chapters that follow, we'll delve deeper into this historic day in Australian racing. We'll explore the race itself, the emotional aftermath, and the lasting impact of Might and Power's Melbourne Cup victory. November 4, 1997, was more than just a race day; it was a moment when a horse became a national hero.

Might and Power's victory in the Melbourne Cup on that historic day was not just about records and titles; it was about the spirit of a champion that defied expectations and showcased the power of belief. It was a reminder that in the world of sports, true greatness is achieved through a combination of talent, dedication, and the unyielding pursuit of excellence. His story was a testament that legends are not born; they are made through hard work, perseverance, and the unwavering belief in the power of a dream.

The Weight of Expectations

As Might and Power stood triumphant in the winner's circle at the 1997 Melbourne Cup, he had achieved a feat that seemed nearly impossible. Carrying 56 kilograms, a weight that hadn't been shouldered to victory in decades, he had not only won Australia's most prestigious race, but he had done so in record-breaking fashion. The nation erupted in celebration, and a new hero was born.

Yet, the weight of expectations on that historic day was more than just a physical burden. It was the weight of history, the weight of hope, and the weight of a nation's dreams. Australians had been yearning for a champion, a horse to rekindle the glory days of Phar Lap, and Might and Power had become the embodiment of those hopes.

In the lead-up to the Melbourne Cup, the anticipation had reached a fever pitch. Racing experts and enthusiasts debated whether he could handle the immense weight, whether he could overcome the challenges of an elite field of competitors, and whether he could live up to the lofty expectations set upon his shoulders.

For trainer Jack Denham and jockey Jim Cassidy, the pressure was immense. They were not only responsible for the physical well-being of the horse but also for ensuring that he was in the right mental state. The horse had to be confident, focused, and determined to rise above the weight and win the race.

Might and Power's preparations were meticulous. His diet, training regimen, and overall care were scrutinized, with every detail examined for potential improvement. The team knew that victory in the Melbourne Cup was not just about talent; it was about perfection in every aspect of his preparation.

As the race day approached, the nation held its collective breath. The Caulfield Cup had been a remarkable triumph, but the Melbourne Cup was the ultimate test. Could he do it again? Could he handle the weight and the expectations?

In the moments leading up to the race, the atmosphere was a mix of excitement and tension. The mounting yard was abuzz, and the crowd was eager to catch a glimpse of the champion. Every move, every twitch of his ears, and every step he took were analyzed for signs of confidence. The eyes of a nation were on him.

When the gates opened, and the field thundered down the straight, it was a moment of truth. Might and Power had to carry not only his physical weight but also the weight of a nation's dreams. The race was a test of character, and he responded with unwavering determination.

As he crossed the finish line, victorious, the weight of expectations turned into a triumphant celebration. Australians from all walks of life cheered for a horse who had defied history and carried their hopes to glory. The burden had become a symbol of the power of belief and the spirit of a champion.

In the chapters that follow, we'll explore the impact of Might and Power's Melbourne Cup victory on the racing world and Australian society. We'll delve into the weight of expectations, the thrill of the race, and the emotional aftermath that defined a historic day.

Might and Power's victory in the Melbourne Cup was not just about records and titles; it was about the spirit of a champion that defied expectations and showcased the power of belief. It was a reminder that in the world of sports, true greatness is achieved not only through physical prowess but through the ability to handle the weight of pressure and rise above it. His story was a testament that legends are not born; they are made through hard work, perseverance, and the unwavering belief in the power of a dream.

Chapter 8: Melbourne's Hero: The Might and Power Saga

The Melbourne Cup Victory

It was a day that would be etched in the annals of Australian racing history, a day when Might and Power became more than just a champion; he became a legend. The first Tuesday in November, 1997, marked a moment when the Melbourne Cup embraced a new hero, and Australia celebrated the triumph of its favorite son.

The Melbourne Cup had always held a special place in the hearts of Australians. It was more than just a horse race; it was a cultural event that united the nation. As the field lined up at the Flemington Racecourse that fateful day, the expectations were higher than ever.

For Might and Power, the Melbourne Cup was the ultimate test of his mettle. The weight of history rested upon his shoulders, quite literally, as he carried 56 kilograms—more than any Melbourne Cup winner in decades. He was not just racing against a field of competitors; he was racing against the ghosts of champions past.

As the starting gates opened, the thundering hooves of the field filled the air, and the nation held its breath. Might and Power, under the guidance of jockey Jim Cassidy, settled into the race. Every stride was a testament to his power and determination.

In the final stretch, as the horses surged toward the finish line, Might and Power made his move. With a burst of speed and a heart filled with determination, he left his competitors in the dust. The roar of the crowd was deafening as he crossed the finish line, securing victory in the Melbourne Cup.

The victory was not just about winning a race; it was about the nation's horse, a horse that had captured the hearts of Australians. Flemington erupted in joy, as fans, punters, and well-wishers celebrated a moment they had longed for.

Might and Power had not only won a prestigious race; he had become the Melbourne Cup champion. He had entered the pantheon of greats, alongside legends like Phar Lap and Kingston Town. His triumph was a testament to the power of belief, the spirit of a champion, and the unyielding determination of a horse who had defied the weight of history.

As he paraded in front of the grandstands, his white blaze gleaming, the cheers and applause were unending. The nation's hero had returned victorious. He had done what many thought was impossible.

In the chapters that follow, we'll delve deeper into the Melbourne Cup victory and its impact on Australian society. We'll explore the emotional aftermath, the recognition and honors that followed, and the enduring legacy of Might and Power.

Might and Power's Melbourne Cup victory was not just about a horse winning a race; it was about a nation finding a hero and a horse who would forever be celebrated as one of the greatest champions in Australian racing history.

The Nation's Horse

When Might and Power crossed the finish line at the 1997 Melbourne Cup, he did more than just win a race; he became a symbol of national pride and unity. The moment he was draped in victory garlands, he transformed into "the nation's horse."

In Australia, the Melbourne Cup has always held a special place in the national psyche. It's a race that stops the nation, where people from all walks of life come together to celebrate a shared love for racing. Yet, the victory of Might and Power in 1997 transcended the boundaries of a mere horse race. He became a horse for the people, a horse who carried the dreams and aspirations of an entire nation.

As the nation's horse, Might and Power represented more than just his owners or the racing industry. He represented a story of hope, resilience, and the triumph of the underdog. Australians, known for their love of sports and their passion for backing the underdog, found a hero in this chestnut colt.

From the moment he set foot on the racetrack, Might and Power embodied the Australian spirit. He was tough, determined, and unyielding, just like the people who cheered for him. He carried the weight of expectations and history with grace and power, a symbol of the can-do attitude that defines the nation.

In the days and weeks following his Melbourne Cup victory, Might and Power's fame transcended the realm of horse racing. He became a household name, his image gracing front pages of newspapers, magazine covers, and television screens. Everyone wanted a piece of the nation's horse, and he graciously accepted the adoration.

The victory tour that followed was a whirlwind of appearances at racetracks, events, and parades. Australians flocked to see him, to touch the horse that had brought the nation to its feet. His presence was not just about racing; it was a celebration of what could be achieved with determination, perseverance, and the belief in oneself.

His story resonated with a diverse audience. The old and the young, the urban and the rural, all found something to admire in Might and Power. He was more than just a racehorse; he was a symbol of Australian identity.

As the nation's horse, he carried the hopes and dreams of Australians to races around the world. His success in prestigious events like the Cox Plate added to his legend. He proved that a horse from down under could take on the world and emerge victorious.

The Melbourne Cup victory of 1997 was a moment when a horse became a national hero. Australians embraced Might and Power, not just as a racehorse, but as a symbol of what it meant to be Australian. He was the embodiment of resilience, the champion of the underdog, and the horse who carried the weight of a nation's expectations with grace and power.

In the chapters that follow, we'll explore the enduring legacy of Might and Power as the nation's horse. We'll delve into his impact on racing, society, and the hearts of those who cheered for him. His story is a testament to the power of sport to unite a nation and the enduring bond between a horse and a people.

Might and Power's journey from a promising colt to the nation's horse is a story of triumph, not just on the racetrack but in the hearts of all who believed in the power of dreams and the spirit of a champion.

Media Frenzy and Public Adoration

After Might and Power's historic Melbourne Cup victory, the nation found itself in the grip of a media frenzy. The story of a horse defying history and carrying 56 kilograms to win Australia's most prestigious race was a narrative that captured the imagination of not only racing enthusiasts but also the broader public. The media played a pivotal role in amplifying the legend of this extraordinary racehorse.

The moment he crossed the finish line, cameras clicked, journalists scribbled furiously, and headlines were crafted in newsrooms across the country. The front pages of newspapers were emblazoned with images of the champion horse and jockey Jim Cassidy. Magazines rushed to feature him on their covers, and television broadcasts were dedicated to reliving the thrilling race.

One of the key factors contributing to the media's fascination with Might and Power was his incredible backstory. His journey from a humble beginning to a Melbourne Cup champion was the stuff of dreams. His owners, Nick and Janice Moraitis, had purchased him for a mere $42,000, making him one of the most affordable horses to achieve such greatness. This rags-to-riches narrative resonated with the Australian public, who saw in him a symbol of hope and possibility.

Media outlets, both print and electronic, scrambled to interview everyone connected to the horse. Trainer Jack Denham and jockey Jim Cassidy became overnight celebrities, their insights into Might and Power's preparation and performance in high demand. The nation wanted to know every detail of how this extraordinary feat had been accomplished.

Might and Power's owner, Nick Moraitis, was thrust into the limelight as well. His passion for horse racing and his belief in this unassuming colt had paid off in the most spectacular fashion. His interviews became a source of inspiration for those who aspired to achieve greatness against the odds.

The public, too, was swept up in a wave of adoration for the horse. People from all walks of life identified with the underdog spirit of Might and Power. He became a symbol of Australian resilience and determination, values that Australians hold dear.

Public appearances by Might and Power drew enormous crowds. Children and adults alike flocked to see him, to touch the mane of a champion, and to bask in the glory of the nation's horse. The scenes were reminiscent of a rock star's tour, and the horse, with his distinctive white blaze, was the star of the show.

As the celebrations continued, Might and Power was showered with honors and accolades. He was named the Australian Horse of the Year, a title that elevated his status to the highest echelons of racing. Awards ceremonies and banquets celebrated his achievements, and his story was immortalized in books, documentaries, and films.

Yet, amid the media frenzy and public adoration, Might and Power remained a horse of remarkable character. He didn't let the newfound fame affect his temperament. His down-to-earth nature and his affinity for hard work endeared him even more to those who had the privilege of meeting him.

In the chapters that follow, we'll delve deeper into the media's role in shaping Might and Power's legacy. We'll explore the impact of his Melbourne Cup victory on Australian society and the enduring adoration that continued throughout his career and beyond.

Might and Power's story was more than a sporting triumph; it was a cultural phenomenon. It was a tale of media frenzy and public adoration, a reminder that the power of belief, when combined with exceptional talent, can transcend the boundaries of sport and capture the hearts of a nation.

A Legend is Born

November 4, 1997, was a day that etched its name in history, and a legend was born. On that glorious Melbourne Cup Day, the nation witnessed the rise of a new hero, a horse who defied the odds, a horse who became more than a champion—he became a legend.

The moment Might and Power thundered down the final stretch at Flemington Racecourse, carrying the hopes and dreams of a nation, he secured a place in Australian folklore. The chestnut colt's triumph in the Melbourne Cup was not just a victory; it was an epic tale of courage, determination, and the unyielding spirit of a horse and its connections.

As he crossed the finish line, the roar of the crowd was deafening. Thousands of spectators had gathered to witness history, to see if the chestnut colt with a distinctive white blaze could accomplish the seemingly impossible. And he did. With each stride, he left his competitors behind, displaying a burst of speed that defied the 56 kilograms he carried. He won by a margin that was as astounding as it was historical.

The moment was pure theater. Jockey Jim Cassidy, known as "Pumper" for his distinctive riding style, celebrated with a triumphant fist pump. The emotions were palpable as he stood in the stirrups, saluting the crowd. The spectators, who had held their breath throughout the race, erupted in joy. The cheers, applause, and jubilation were unparalleled. It was a moment of collective euphoria, a moment that united a nation.

For Might and Power, the victory wasn't just about winning a race; it was about carrying the hopes of an entire nation. He became the hero Australians had been waiting for, the underdog who had defied the weight of history and the expectations that came with it.

The media, in its frenzy, was quick to christen him as "the people's horse." His victory was a symbol of Australian spirit, a testament to the belief that anyone, or in this case, any horse, could rise above challenges and succeed.

The legend of Might and Power was more than just a Melbourne Cup victory. It was a tale of inspiration, of a nation's hero, and of a horse who had captured the hearts of millions. The images of that historic day became iconic, forever etched in the memories of those who witnessed it.

In the days and weeks that followed, Might and Power continued to bask in the limelight. The public adoration showed no signs of waning. He made appearances at racetracks, events, and parades, where thousands came to catch a glimpse of the champion. His story wasn't just about racing; it was about the belief in the power of dreams and the spirit of a champion.

As we explore the legend of Might and Power in the chapters that follow, we'll delve deeper into the Melbourne Cup victory and its impact on Australian society. We'll examine the emotional aftermath, the recognition and honors that followed, and the enduring legacy of this iconic racehorse.

Might and Power's victory was a defining moment in Australian racing, a moment when a legend was born, a moment that would forever be etched in the nation's collective memory.

Chapter 9: Triple Crown Pursuit: Might and Power's Victorious Year

Conquering Major Races

After the historic triumph at the 1997 Melbourne Cup, the racing world had its eyes firmly set on Might and Power. The chestnut colt had not only secured his place in Australian racing lore but had also announced himself as a contender on the global stage. His journey was far from over, and in the following year, he embarked on a campaign that would see him conquer major races and continue to etch his name in the annals of horse racing history.

The year 1998 would become a defining one for Might and Power and his connections. The colt was at the peak of his career, and his trainers and jockey knew that they had a once-in-a-lifetime horse in their stable. The Triple Crown, consisting of the Cox Plate, the Caulfield Cup, and the Melbourne Cup, was the next challenge on the horizon, and the team was determined to capture it.

The first leg of the Triple Crown, the Cox Plate, was an opportunity for Might and Power to prove his mettle. Historically, the Cox Plate had been considered one of the most prestigious weight-for-age races in Australia. To secure a victory here meant that the colt was not just a stayer but also a versatile horse capable of triumphing in different racing conditions.

Might and Power did not disappoint. In an outstanding display of his abilities, he cruised to victory in the Cox Plate, adding another jewel to his already impressive crown. The victory marked him as one of the finest racehorses Australia had ever seen.

With the Cox Plate secured, attention turned to the Caulfield Cup, the second leg of the Triple Crown. Winning both the Cox Plate and the Caulfield Cup had been a rare feat, and Might and Power was poised to achieve it. Yet, the Caulfield Cup posed its own set of challenges, including a handicap format that made the race a true test of a horse's ability to carry weight.

Once again, Might and Power defied expectations and powered to victory in the Caulfield Cup. His remarkable performances in these two races not only showcased his versatility but also demonstrated his exceptional talent in the face of challenging conditions.

With the first two legs of the Triple Crown in the bag, the final test was the Melbourne Cup. No horse had won all three races in a single year since the legendary Phar Lap in 1930. The weight of history and expectations was immense, but if there was one horse capable of achieving the Triple Crown, it was Might and Power.

The buildup to the Melbourne Cup was filled with anticipation and excitement. The nation held its breath as the colt prepared to carry a record weight of 56 kilograms in the race. It was a weight that had historically been insurmountable for most horses. But Might and Power was no ordinary horse.

On the first Tuesday in November 1998, history was made once again. Might and Power stormed to victory in the Melbourne Cup, becoming the first horse in 68 years to achieve the Triple Crown. The nation erupted in jubilation, celebrating not just a victory but a feat that might never be repeated in their lifetime.

The journey from the Melbourne Cup of 1997 to the Triple Crown of 1998 was a testament to the exceptional talent of Might and Power and the unwavering determination of his connections. He had not only conquered major races, but he had also secured a place among the greatest racehorses in history.

In the chapters that follow, we'll explore the individual races that made up the Triple Crown, the challenges faced, and the emotions that accompanied each victory. Might and Power's Triple Crown pursuit was a year to remember, a year of triumph, and a year that would forever be etched in the racing annals as a testament to the power and grace of a champion.

Unforgettable Moments

The year 1998 will forever be etched in the annals of Australian horse racing history. It was the year of Might and Power, a colt whose name became synonymous with victory, courage, and the unrelenting pursuit of greatness. As he embarked on his Triple Crown pursuit, he left an indelible mark on the hearts of racing enthusiasts and a nation in awe.

Might and Power's journey to the Triple Crown was more than a series of races; it was a narrative filled with unforgettable moments that defined the spirit of this extraordinary racehorse.

The Cox Plate Glory: The first leg of the Triple Crown was the Cox Plate, a race often referred to as the "Race Where Legends Are Made." It was here that Might and Power would take his first step toward achieving a feat not seen in nearly seven decades. The race was a test of speed, stamina, and versatility, and the colt proved himself to be a true champion. The moment he surged ahead to cross the finish line was a breathtaking sight, a moment that would be replayed in racing history documentaries for years to come.

Triumph in the Caulfield Cup: The Caulfield Cup was the next challenge, and it carried its own set of hurdles. Handicap races demanded a horse's ability to carry weight, and Might and Power was tasked with carrying 58 kilograms.

It was a daunting challenge, but the colt, with his indomitable spirit, prevailed. The victory not only showcased his versatility but also underlined his exceptional talent. It was a day that left fans in awe, and they celebrated their hero with unrivaled enthusiasm.

The Melbourne Cup Magic: The final leg of the Triple Crown was the Melbourne Cup, a race that had become an inseparable part of Australia's cultural fabric. It was the race where history was made, and Might and Power aimed to etch his name among the immortals of the sport. Carrying a record weight of 56 kilograms, the odds were stacked against him. However, the nation's faith in their hero was unwavering. When he crossed the line to become the first horse in 68 years to win the Triple Crown, it was a moment of pure magic. The cheers of the crowd, the tears in the eyes of his connections, and the joy that swept the nation were unforgettable.

The Embrace of a Nation: Might and Power's victories were not just about his raw talent; they were about the unbreakable bond he formed with the Australian people. His triumphs transcended the realm of sports and became a source of national pride. He was a horse who had carried the dreams of a nation on his back, and the nation responded with unwavering support and admiration. His races became events where people from all walks of life gathered to witness history. The moments of collective euphoria, when the nation celebrated his victories, were unforgettable. The chants of "Mighty, Mighty" echoed through racetracks, and the colt became an embodiment of the Australian spirit.

The Tribute to a Champion: In the aftermath of the Triple Crown, tributes and honors poured in. Might and Power was named the Australian Horse of the Year, and his legacy was celebrated through awards and accolades. His story became a subject of books, documentaries, and films. The narrative of a horse who had defied history resonated with people around the world, and his name became synonymous with victory and the pursuit of dreams.

The Legacy Continues: The unforgettable moments of 1998 were not the end of Might and Power's story; they were the continuation of a legacy. As he carried the Triple Crown, he also carried the hopes and aspirations of a nation. His name would forever be whispered with reverence, his victories celebrated as the embodiment of the Australian spirit.

In the chapters that follow, we'll delve into the individual races that made up the Triple Crown and explore the challenges faced, the emotions experienced, and the indomitable spirit of a champion. Might and Power's 1998 campaign was more than a year of victories; it was a year of unforgettable moments that would forever be etched in the memories of those who had the privilege of witnessing his greatness.

Racing's Golden Year

The year 1998 would forever be remembered as the golden year of Australian horse racing. It was a year that saw the emergence of a legend, the triumph of an underdog, and a display of sheer determination and exceptional talent. It was the year of Might and Power, a year that would become the stuff of racing folklore.

The Triple Crown Pursuit: As the year began, the stage was set for an audacious quest. Might and Power, fresh from his historic Melbourne Cup victory in 1997, embarked on a journey that would capture the imagination of a nation. The Triple Crown—a challenge that had not been conquered in nearly seven decades—loomed on the horizon. It consisted of the Cox Plate, the Caulfield Cup, and the Melbourne Cup, three prestigious races that demanded a horse's versatility, stamina, and sheer class.

The Cox Plate was the first hurdle, and it was a test that Might and Power passed with flying colors. He dominated the field, showcasing his speed and tenacity. The nation was awestruck as he added another jewel to his crown. The Caulfield Cup was next, and it brought its own set of challenges. Handicap racing required a horse to carry weight, and he was tasked with a daunting 58 kilograms. Yet, once again, he triumphed, solidifying his status as an exceptional athlete.

The final leg of the Triple Crown was the Melbourne Cup, a race that held a special place in the hearts of all Australians. Carrying a record weight of 56 kilograms, he defied history and the weight of expectations to emerge victorious. The nation celebrated not just a win but a historic achievement that might never be repeated.

Conquering Major Races: The Triple Crown pursuit was not the only highlight of Might and Power's golden year. He conquered major races with an ease that was both astonishing and inspiring. His performances in the lead-up to the Melbourne Cup were awe-inspiring, leaving no doubt that he was a horse destined for greatness.

He added the Tancred Stakes, the Mercedes Classic, and the Queen Elizabeth Stakes to his list of victories. Each race showcased his versatility and power. The Tancred Stakes victory was particularly memorable, as it came on the heels of his Melbourne Cup triumph, highlighting his ability to maintain peak form.

The Australian Horse of the Year: The accolades poured in for Might and Power. He was rightfully crowned the Australian Horse of the Year, a title that reflected his dominance on the racetrack and his status as a national hero.

The award was a fitting tribute to a horse who had captured the hearts of the nation and had achieved the extraordinary.

The Spirit of a Champion: What made Might and Power's golden year truly exceptional was not just the victories but the spirit he embodied. He was more than a racehorse; he was a symbol of resilience, determination, and the unyielding pursuit of dreams. He became known as "the people's horse," a title he wore with grace and humility. His story transcended the realm of sports and became a source of inspiration for people from all walks of life.

The Legacy of 1998: Might and Power's golden year left an indelible mark on Australian racing. His legacy continued to inspire generations of racegoers, trainers, and jockeys. His name became synonymous with courage and triumph, and his story was told and retold as an example of what could be achieved with unwavering determination.

In the chapters that follow, we will delve into the individual races that made up this golden year, the challenges faced, and the emotions experienced. Might and Power's 1998 campaign was more than a year of victories; it was a testament to the spirit of a champion and the enduring magic of horse racing.

Defying the Odds

The year 1998 was a year of dreams, and at the heart of those dreams stood a horse named Might and Power. His pursuit of the elusive Triple Crown was a story of determination, resilience, and an unwavering belief in the face of overwhelming odds.

Triple Crown: A Historic Challenge: The Triple Crown had not been achieved in nearly seven decades when Might and Power and his connections decided to take on the challenge. It consisted of three prestigious races—the Cox Plate, the Caulfield Cup, and the Melbourne Cup. To succeed in the Triple Crown, a horse needed to possess a unique blend of speed, stamina, and versatility. It was a task that had daunted many before, but Might and Power's team believed they had a horse capable of defying the odds.

The Cox Plate Triumph: The journey began with the Cox Plate, a race known as the "Race Where Legends Are Made." The field was strong, and many believed that Might and Power might find it difficult to compete with the seasoned veterans. But what unfolded on the racetrack was nothing short of extraordinary. Might and Power surged ahead with a breathtaking display of speed and tenacity, leaving his competitors in his wake. The odds were defied, and he was on the path to history.

The Weight of Expectations: The Caulfield Cup posed a different challenge—handicap racing. It required horses to carry weights determined by their past performances. Might and Power was assigned a daunting 58 kilograms, the heaviest weight for a three-year-old in more than two decades. The weight of expectations was as heavy as the burden he carried. Yet, he defied the odds once more, showcasing his strength and resilience as he crossed the finish line first.

Melbourne Cup: A Record Weight: The Melbourne Cup, the final leg of the Triple Crown, was where the odds seemed almost insurmountable. Carrying a record weight of 56 kilograms, Might and Power was tasked with rewriting history. The weight of history and expectations rested on his broad shoulders, and many questioned whether he could withstand the challenge. Once again, the odds were defied. In front of a jubilant crowd, Might and Power powered to victory, becoming the first horse in 68 years to achieve the Triple Crown.

The Nation's Hero: The victories in the Triple Crown were not just about horse racing; they were about a nation's spirit. Might and Power had become more than a racehorse; he was a symbol of defiance in the face of overwhelming odds. His achievements inspired people across Australia and beyond, reinforcing the belief that with determination and heart, anything was possible.

The Legacy of Defying the Odds: Might and Power's journey in 1998 became a symbol of triumph against adversity. His story continued to inspire generations of horse racing enthusiasts and anyone who dared to dream big. The odds that he defied were not just the weight on his back; they were the expectations and doubts that he shattered with each victory.

In the chapters that follow, we'll explore Might and Power's individual races during his Triple Crown pursuit, each a testament to his extraordinary ability to overcome the odds. His 1998 campaign was more than a year of victories; it was a year of defying the odds and rewriting the history of Australian horse racing.

Chapter 10: Ownership Shift: The Turning Point for Might and Power

A New Owner, a New Chapter

The year 1998 had been a triumphant journey for Might and Power, but it was also a turning point. After a historic Triple Crown campaign, a significant change in ownership would shape the future of the champion racehorse.

The Old Guard: Under the ownership of Nick Moraitis, Might and Power had achieved remarkable success. Together with trainer Jack Denham and jockey Jim Cassidy, the team had guided the horse to victory in some of Australia's most prestigious races. However, the world of horse racing is dynamic, and ownership changes are not uncommon.

The Sale: In a move that took the racing world by surprise, Nick Moraitis made the decision to sell Might and Power. The news sent shockwaves through the industry, leaving many to wonder what the future held for the beloved champion. The sale marked the end of an era and the beginning of a new chapter.

A New Owner Emerges: The horse's fate hung in the balance until a new owner stepped into the picture. Malaysian businessman Tan Sri Vincent Tan, known for his involvement in various industries, including horse racing, saw the potential in Might and Power. He believed the horse still had more to give to the sport and the racing world. The transition of ownership took place, and the champion found himself in new hands.

Challenges and Expectations: A change in ownership brought with it a new set of challenges and expectations. For Tan Sri Vincent Tan, the pressure was on to continue the legacy of success that Might and Power had established. Fans, too, wondered whether the horse could maintain his peak form under new ownership.

From Might to Power: The change in ownership also coincided with a change in the horse's name. Previously known simply as "Might," he was renamed "Power" under his new ownership. The name change symbolized a shift in the journey, but it was also met with mixed emotions from those who had followed his career as "Might."

Challenges and Opportunities: For Tan Sri Vincent Tan, taking ownership of Might and Power was not just a financial investment; it was a passion project. He was determined to continue the horse's success while ensuring his well-being. Challenges such as adapting to new training methods and managing the expectations of fans and the racing community lay ahead.

The Turning Point: The transition of ownership marked a significant turning point in Might and Power's career. It was a moment that would shape the horse's future and determine whether he could continue to excel on the racetrack. As the spotlight shifted from Nick Moraitis to Tan Sri Vincent Tan, the world watched with bated breath to see what the next chapter held for this beloved champion.

In the chapters that follow, we'll explore the challenges and triumphs that Might and Power faced under his new ownership. The horse's journey continued to be a source of inspiration and intrigue, with a fresh chapter yet to be written in his remarkable story.

Change of Fortunes

The transition in ownership marked a turning point in the journey of Might and Power. Under the guidance of new owner Tan Sri Vincent Tan, the champion racehorse embarked on a path that would come to define the next phase of his remarkable career.

New Beginnings: As the horse formerly known as "Might" became "Power" under his new ownership, it signified more than just a name change. It was the dawn of a new era, a fresh beginning that brought with it both opportunities and challenges. Fans and racing enthusiasts were eager to see how the champion would perform under these new circumstances.

Training and Adaptation: With a new owner came new perspectives and approaches to training. The horse was entrusted to a team that was determined to ensure his continued success on the racetrack. Training methods, routines, and strategies were adjusted to align with the champion's potential. Adapting to these changes would be crucial for his future performances.

The Weight of Expectations: While the horse's new ownership brought a sense of rejuvenation, it also carried with it the weight of expectations. Might and Power had already achieved legendary status, and the racing world anticipated his every move. Fans and enthusiasts wondered if he could maintain his peak form, especially in the face of evolving competition.

Continuing the Legacy: Tan Sri Vincent Tan was keenly aware of the legacy he inherited when he took ownership of the champion. He was committed not only to continuing the legacy but also to enhancing it. The stakes were high, and the pressure to succeed in the world of horse racing was unrelenting.

Challenges on the Horizon: The path forward was not without its challenges. Might and Power was no longer the young colt who had burst onto the scene. With age came the natural wear and tear of a racing career. Injuries and setbacks were part and parcel of the sport, and both the owner and the horse had to face these challenges with resilience and determination.

Retaining Dominance: As the new chapter in Might and Power's career unfolded, the question that loomed large was whether he could retain his dominance in Australian horse racing. The landscape had evolved, and younger talents emerged on the scene, posing a formidable challenge to the champion's reign.

The Journey Continues: Despite the changes in ownership, name, and training, one thing remained constant—the indomitable spirit of Might and Power. He was more than a racehorse; he was a symbol of resilience and the unyielding pursuit of greatness. The journey continued, and the world watched with anticipation as the champion raced into the next chapter of his extraordinary career.

In the chapters that follow, we'll delve into the challenges and triumphs that Might and Power faced under his new ownership. The horse's journey remained a testament to the enduring magic of horse racing and the unwavering spirit of a true champion.

Might Becomes Power

With a change in ownership came a change in identity. The horse that had captured the hearts of racing enthusiasts as "Might" was reborn as "Power" under the ownership of Tan Sri Vincent Tan. This transformation was more than a mere alteration of name; it marked the next phase in the journey of this champion racehorse.

The Renaming: The decision to rename a legendary racehorse is a significant one. In the case of "Might and Power," the transition from "Might" to "Power" represented a fresh start. The change was not arbitrary; it signified a shift in ownership, direction, and perspective. Fans and the racing community greeted the new name with a mixture of curiosity and nostalgia.

The Legacy of "Might": "Might" had become a household name. The horse had dominated the Australian racing scene, securing victories in prestigious events and etching his name in the annals of horse racing history. "Might" was synonymous with power, speed, and resilience. The change to "Power" brought with it the weight of expectations, as fans wondered whether the horse could live up to his former self.

A New Identity: As "Power," the horse embarked on a journey to redefine his identity on the racetrack. The name was not the only thing that changed; there were shifts in training methods, strategies, and even racing objectives. The transformation was a testament to the commitment of Tan Sri Vincent Tan and his team to harness the full potential of this exceptional athlete.

The Challenges of Transition: A change in identity and ownership was not without its challenges. Horses, like humans, have their unique personalities and temperaments. Adjusting to new surroundings, trainers, and routines can be a testing experience. The bond between horse and owner, which plays a vital role in racing success, needed to be rebuilt from the ground up.

The Unwavering Spirit: Despite the changes, one thing remained constant—Power's unwavering spirit. He had displayed courage and determination throughout his career, and these qualities were not diminished by the alterations. The horse's heart and tenacity were qualities that made him a champion, regardless of the name he carried.

A Horse by Any Other Name: As the racing world adjusted to the transformation, the essence of the horse remained unchanged. The name on the race card might have shifted from "Might" to "Power," but the thrill of watching him compete, the roar of the crowd, and the exhilaration of victory were still very much the same.

The Beginning of a New Era: "Might Becomes Power" was not just a change in identity; it was the dawn of a new era in the champion's career. Under the ownership of Tan Sri Vincent Tan, the horse would continue to strive for greatness and secure his place in the annals of Australian horse racing history.

In the chapters that follow, we'll delve deeper into the challenges and triumphs that defined this new phase of Power's career. The horse's journey continued to be a symbol of the enduring spirit of horse racing and the indomitable will of a true champion.

Challenges on the Horizon

As "Might" transitioned into "Power" under new ownership, the champion racehorse faced a series of challenges that would test his mettle and determination. The journey under the guidance of Tan Sri Vincent Tan came with hurdles that needed to be overcome.

The Weight of Expectations: With a new name and a new owner, "Power" carried with him the weight of expectations. The racing community and fans anticipated his every race with bated breath. The champion's previous achievements had set the bar exceptionally high, and many wondered if he could continue to deliver at the same level. This added pressure created a unique challenge for both the horse and his new owner.

The Test of Adaptation: Horses, like all athletes, develop routines and habits that suit their individual needs. A change in ownership often necessitates adjustments in training methods and schedules. "Power" had to adapt to a new training regimen, new trainers, and new surroundings. It was a transition that required both physical and mental adjustments.

Age and Wear: The relentless nature of horse racing takes its toll on even the most exceptional athletes. "Power" was no longer the young colt that had burst onto the racing scene. His body bore the signs of his racing career, with the wear and tear of competition showing. Managing the horse's fitness and health became an essential aspect of the challenge.

Competition's Evolution: The racing landscape had evolved since "Power's" earlier victories. Younger, talented horses had emerged on the scene, presenting a formidable challenge. Racing is a highly competitive sport, and each new generation of horses pushes the boundaries of what is achievable. The question of whether "Power" could maintain his dominance was ever-present.

Injuries and Setbacks: In the world of horse racing, injuries are an unfortunate reality. The physical demands of racing can lead to strains, sprains, and more serious injuries. "Power" was not immune to these setbacks, and his resilience was tested as he recovered from injuries. The horse's ability to bounce back from adversity would be a crucial aspect of his journey.

The Bond with a New Owner: The relationship between a horse and its owner is an essential element in racing success. Tan Sri Vincent Tan and "Power" needed to establish their bond from the ground up. Building trust, understanding the horse's cues, and developing effective communication were part of the challenge.

Resilience and Determination: The essence of a champion is often defined by their ability to overcome obstacles and emerge stronger. "Power" had already displayed remarkable resilience and determination in his career. The challenges on the horizon would test these qualities once more and reveal the true depth of his spirit.

As we delve deeper into "Power's" journey under new ownership, we'll explore how he faced and overcame these challenges. The next chapter in his extraordinary career was marked by both hurdles and triumphs, making it a testament to the enduring magic of horse racing and the unwavering spirit of a true champion.

Chapter 11: Battles and Victories: The Year of Resilience

Facing Adversity

The year that unfolded under the banner of "Power" proved to be a year of resilience. As the champion racehorse continued his journey under new ownership, he encountered various adversities that tested the depth of his character. The challenges he faced in this period were as formidable as any he had encountered on the racetrack.

Injury Strikes: Adversity came swiftly in the form of injuries. Horses, no matter how strong or skilled, are susceptible to the physical strains of racing. "Power" was no exception. The season was marked by injuries that threatened to sideline the champion. It was a moment that forced the entire team to confront the harsh reality of the sport.

The Rehabilitation Process: Recovery from injuries is an intricate and demanding process for a racehorse. It involves not only physical healing but also the psychological challenge of returning to peak performance. The journey of rehabilitation was marked by hard work, dedication, and patience. "Power" had to trust in the expertise of his trainers and the resilience of his own body.

The Psychological Toll: Adversity does not only manifest physically but also takes a toll on the mental state of an athlete, even one as noble as a racehorse. The frustration of not being able to compete, the uncertainty of recovery, and the fear of setbacks were all elements that "Power" had to grapple with. His journey through these mental challenges was a testament to his character.

The Decision-Making Process: During this period, critical decisions had to be made. The owners, trainers, and veterinary experts had to weigh the risks and benefits of returning "Power" to the racetrack. The decisions made were pivotal in shaping the champion's future. The horse's welfare was paramount, and every choice was made with his best interests at heart.

The Comeback Trail: "Power's" return to the racetrack was a moment of triumph. It represented not only the recovery of a remarkable athlete but also a symbol of hope and resilience. The anticipation and excitement among fans were palpable. The champion's performance upon his return was a testament to his indomitable spirit.

Hard-Won Victories: The year of adversity was also a year of hard-won victories. Each race carried with it the weight of the challenges "Power" had faced. The triumphs were not just in the victories themselves but in the journey that led to those moments. These races were a testament to the champion's courage, determination, and the unwavering support of his team.

The Resilience of a Champion: The adversities of this year showcased the true spirit of a champion. "Power" had already proven his mettle on the racetrack, but this period revealed a depth of character that extended beyond winning. It was a story of resilience, fortitude, and the enduring bond between a horse and its team.

In the chapters that follow, we'll delve deeper into the triumphs and challenges of this remarkable year. The horse's journey through adversity was a testament to the enduring magic of horse racing and the indomitable will of a true champion.

The Courage to Fight

In the face of adversity, champions are defined not by the absence of challenges but by their unwavering courage to confront and conquer them. "Power" embodied this courage as he embarked on a year of resilience marked by injuries and setbacks. The journey through these hardships revealed the indomitable spirit of a true champion.

The Battle Begins: The year of resilience kicked off with a setback that tested "Power" and his team. Injuries had become an unwanted companion, threatening to derail the champion's career. It was a moment that demanded courage and conviction to face the road ahead.

A Champion's Mindset: Champions possess a unique mindset. They view challenges as opportunities, adversity as a chance to showcase their mettle, and setbacks as a prelude to comebacks. "Power" embraced this mindset as he faced his injuries head-on.

The Rehabilitation Challenge: The path to recovery was fraught with challenges. Rehabilitation is not only a physical journey but a mental one. "Power" had to muster the courage to endure the grueling process of healing and training, often in the face of discomfort and uncertainty.

The Team's Support: Courage is not a solitary endeavor. The support of trainers, veterinarians, owners, and a dedicated team was integral to "Power's" journey. Their unwavering belief in the champion, their expertise, and their tireless efforts were the pillars of his courage.

Returning to the Track: The day of "Power's" return to the racetrack was a momentous one. It was a day marked by the culmination of courage, resilience, and a relentless pursuit of greatness. Fans watched with bated breath, aware of the challenges that had been overcome.

Overcoming Doubts: The comeback was not without doubts. Skeptics wondered if "Power" could regain his former glory after the trials of injuries. The champion's courage extended to silencing the skeptics and proving that he was a force to be reckoned with.

Triumph Amid Adversity: The races that followed were a showcase of "Power's" courage. Each victory represented a triumph not just over competitors on the track but over the adversities that had threatened to extinguish his career. The champion's courage shone brightly, illuminating the path forward.

An Enduring Spirit: The year of resilience left an indelible mark on "Power." It showcased his courage to fight, his determination to overcome, and his unwavering spirit. The champion's legacy extended beyond victories; it was a testament to the essence of courage.

In the chapters that follow, we'll delve deeper into the victories that defined this remarkable year. The horse's journey through adversity and his unwavering courage were a testament to the enduring magic of horse racing and the indomitable will of a true champion.

The Power to Persist

Resilience is not just about bouncing back from adversity; it's also about the ability to persist through challenging times. "Power" demonstrated this power of persistence as he navigated the trials of injuries and setbacks, emerging stronger and more determined than ever.

The Persistence of a Champion: "Power" had already established himself as a champion on the racetrack, but the year of resilience would test his capacity for persistence. The determination to overcome injuries and setbacks was a testament to the champion's spirit.

A Journey of Small Steps: The road to recovery was marked by small but significant steps. Each day presented new challenges and incremental progress. "Power" exhibited the power of persistence by facing these challenges with unwavering determination.

The Patience of a Team: Persistence was not solely the domain of the champion; it extended to his entire team. Trainers, veterinarians, owners, and jockeys all displayed the patience and commitment necessary to support "Power" on his journey. Their belief in the horse's potential was integral to the process.

The Return to Racing: One of the most significant markers of "Power's" persistence was his return to the racetrack. It was a moment that illustrated the champion's ability to persist through adversity and emerge stronger. The anticipation and excitement were palpable.

Setting New Goals: Persistence often involves setting new goals and pushing the boundaries of what is achievable. "Power" and his team redefined their goals in the face of adversity, aiming not just for victories but for a legacy that would endure.

Resilience in the Spotlight: The races that followed showcased "Power's" resilience in the spotlight. His ability to persist through physical discomfort and mental challenges was evident in each stride. The champion's performances were a testament to the power of persistence.

The Legacy of Persistence: The year of resilience left an enduring legacy. It showcased not only the champion's victories but also his power to persist through adversity. "Power's" story became a symbol of the indomitable spirit of a true champion.

In the chapters that follow, we'll delve deeper into the year that tested "Power's" capacity for persistence. His journey through challenges and setbacks was a testament to the enduring magic of horse racing and the indomitable will of a true champion.

Hard-Won Victories

The year of resilience for "Power" was not just marked by his ability to persist through adversity; it was also characterized by the hard-won victories that defined his journey. Each race carried with it the weight of the challenges he had faced and the triumphs that had eluded him.

The Return to Racing: "Power's" comeback to the racetrack was a victory in itself. It was a moment that had been uncertain, a moment that the entire team had worked tirelessly to achieve. The champion's ability to stand once more in the starting gates was a victory over injuries and setbacks.

The First Triumph: The first race back after his injuries was a defining moment. It was a triumph not just in terms of the finish line but in the courage displayed. "Power" and his jockey demonstrated their unshakable spirit and desire to win.

Conquering Doubts: Skeptics had cast doubt on whether "Power" could regain his former glory. Every victory silenced the naysayers and proved that the champion was more than capable of competing at the highest level. It was a triumph over doubt and skepticism.

Challenges on the Track: The races of the year were not without challenges. Competitors brought their A-game, knowing that defeating "Power" would be a crowning achievement. Each victory on the track was a hard-fought battle, a testament to the champion's tenacity.

Breaking Records: "Power's" victories during this year often came with record-breaking performances. The champion didn't just win; he set new standards and milestones. Each record broken was a victory not only for the horse but for the sport itself.

Defying the Odds: The year of resilience was marked by moments when the odds seemed stacked against "Power." Whether it was the competition, the weight of expectations, or the challenges of recovery, the champion defied these odds to emerge victorious.

The Power of Teamwork: The victories were not just about "Power" but also about the collective effort of his team. Trainers, jockeys, owners, and supporters played an integral role in every victory. Their teamwork was a victory in itself.

An Enduring Legacy: The year of hard-won victories left an enduring legacy. It was a year that showcased the champion's ability to overcome, to rise above adversity, and to secure victories that would be etched in racing history.

In the chapters that follow, we'll delve deeper into the hard-won victories that defined this remarkable year. "Power's" journey through adversity and the triumphs that accompanied it were a testament to the enduring magic of horse racing and the indomitable will of a true champion.

Chapter 12: Guiding Light: John Wheeler and Might and Power's Journey
Transition in Training

John Wheeler, a name synonymous with excellence in horse training, played a pivotal role in "Power's" journey during the year of resilience. The transition in training that the champion underwent marked a crucial phase in his remarkable comeback.

The Trainer's Influence: John Wheeler, a seasoned and respected figure in the world of horse racing, brought his expertise and unique approach to "Power's" training. The transition in training began with Wheeler's influence, as he recognized the potential in the champion.

A New Regimen: Wheeler's training regimen was a departure from the norm. It was tailored to "Power's" specific needs, considering his injuries and the challenges he had faced. This transition involved a shift in routines and practices, all aimed at bringing out the best in the champion.

Physical Rehabilitation: The transition included an intense phase of physical rehabilitation. "Power" had to regain his strength and stamina, and Wheeler's training played a crucial role in this process. It was a transition that demanded resilience and dedication from both horse and trainer.

Mental Resilience: Training is not just about physical conditioning but also mental resilience. "Power" needed to regain his confidence and mental fortitude. The transition in training involved techniques to boost the champion's mental strength, allowing him to face the challenges on the track.

The Return to Racing: The transition culminated in the champion's return to racing. Wheeler's training had prepared "Power" for this moment, instilling in him the skills and confidence necessary to compete at the highest level. It was a transition that showcased the effectiveness of Wheeler's methods.

The Role of the Team: The transition in training was a collaborative effort. Wheeler worked closely with the rest of the team, including veterinarians and jockeys, to ensure that "Power" was in the best possible condition. The champion's journey was a testament to the power of teamwork.

The Spirit Reborn: As "Power" stepped onto the track for his first race after the transition in training, it was clear that he had undergone a transformation. The champion's spirit had been reborn, and his performances reflected the effectiveness of the training under Wheeler's guidance.

Legacy of Training: The transition in training marked a turning point in "Power's" journey. It left an enduring legacy, showcasing the importance of adaptive training in the face of challenges. The champion's successes were a testament to the impact of Wheeler's expertise.

In the chapters that follow, we'll delve deeper into the influence of training and the transformation it brought about in "Power." The champion's journey through adversity and the role of his trainer were integral to his remarkable resurgence.

Wheeler's Influence

In the world of horse racing, the name John Wheeler is synonymous with wisdom, experience, and an innate understanding of these magnificent animals. Wheeler's influence on "Power" during the year of resilience was nothing short of transformative. This section delves into the profound impact that this legendary trainer had on the champion.

The Art of Equine Understanding: John Wheeler's journey with horses is a testament to his unique ability to understand these animals. His deep appreciation for their psychology, personality, and physicality allowed him to tailor training methods specific to each horse. Wheeler's influence on "Power" began with this understanding.

Recognizing Untapped Potential: What set Wheeler apart as a trainer was his ability to recognize untapped potential. He saw in "Power" not just a champion but a horse capable of defying the odds and making a remarkable comeback. Wheeler's influence was rooted in his belief in the horse's ability.

The Transition in Training: Wheeler's influence on "Power" extended to the critical transition in training. He devised a regimen that was customized to address the champion's unique needs. This included rehabilitation exercises, conditioning routines, and a meticulous approach to building the horse's strength.

Guiding Mental Resilience: Training champions isn't just about physical conditioning; it's about fostering mental resilience. Wheeler's influence extended to instilling a sense of confidence and determination in "Power." The champion needed to regain his mental strength, and Wheeler's methods played a pivotal role in this aspect.

Collaboration and Teamwork: Wheeler's influence was marked by his collaborative approach. He worked closely with the rest of the team, including veterinarians and jockeys, to ensure that "Power" received comprehensive care. The unity of the team under Wheeler's guidance was a vital component of the champion's resurgence.

A Return to Racing: The culmination of Wheeler's influence was the champion's return to racing. Under Wheeler's guidance, "Power" was not just physically prepared but mentally ready to compete at the highest level. The trainer's impact on this moment was profound and transformative.

The Legacy of a Trainer: The enduring legacy of Wheeler's influence on "Power" extended beyond the races. It demonstrated the invaluable role of a skilled trainer in a champion's journey. Wheeler's influence became a symbol of the bond between horse and trainer, a testament to the magic of horse racing.

In the chapters that follow, we'll continue to explore the profound impact of John Wheeler's influence on "Power." The trainer's wisdom, experience, and belief in the champion were integral to his resurgence, and the story of their partnership is one of the most compelling narratives in the world of horse racing.

Regaining the Magic

The year of resilience for "Power" was not just a tale of physical recovery; it was also a story of rediscovering the magic that had made the champion a force to be reckoned with. This section explores how, under John Wheeler's guidance, "Power" managed to recapture the essence of his greatness.

The Fading Spark: In the wake of injuries and setbacks, "Power's" spark had dulled. The magic that once defined his racing style and captured the hearts of fans seemed elusive. The champion's journey of regaining the magic began with a recognition of what had been lost.

Trainer's Intuition: John Wheeler's intuitive understanding of horses played a crucial role in regaining the magic. He recognized that the champion's brilliance was still there, waiting to be reignited. Wheeler's ability to communicate with "Power" on a profound level was central to this process.

Tailored Training Techniques: The training techniques employed by Wheeler were tailored to elicit the champion's best qualities. It wasn't about making "Power" something he wasn't; it was about allowing him to be the best version of himself. The training was designed to rekindle the magic that set him apart.

The Champion's Response: As "Power" responded to Wheeler's training, the magic began to resurface. It was evident in his strides, his performances, and his interactions with those around him. The champion's renewed confidence and spirit were emblematic of the magic's return.

The Moments of Brilliance: Races during this phase were marked by moments of sheer brilliance. "Power" seemed to recapture the magic with every victory. His signature moves, his extraordinary speed, and his innate understanding of the track all bore witness to the rekindled magic.

The Spirit Reborn: It wasn't just about winning; it was about winning with the same magic that had defined "Power" at the peak of his career. The champion's spirit was reborn, and it shone brightly on the track, reminding fans of what had made him a legend.

A Legacy of Magic: The legacy of regaining the magic wasn't just about "Power." It was a testament to the enduring enchantment of horse racing itself. The champion's journey through adversity, guided by Wheeler, became a symbol of the magic that keeps fans coming back to the sport.

In the chapters that follow, we'll delve deeper into the moments when the magic returned to "Power" and how this transformation defined the champion's resurgence. The story is one of redemption, rediscovery, and the indomitable spirit of a true racing legend.

The Spirit Reborn

In the midst of adversity and uncertainty, "Power" experienced a profound transformation. This section explores how the champion's spirit, under the guidance of John Wheeler, underwent a rebirth, marking a pivotal moment in his journey.

The Shadows of Doubt: The period of injury and rehabilitation had cast shadows of doubt over "Power's" racing career. His struggles on the track and the questions surrounding his ability had become a looming presence. The spirit reborn began with the courage to face these doubts head-on.

The Trainer's Belief: John Wheeler's unwavering belief in "Power" played a central role in rekindling the champion's spirit. The trainer's words of encouragement and support became a powerful source of motivation. His belief echoed in the champion's every step.

Resilience in the Face of Adversity: "Power's" journey during this phase was a testament to his resilience. The champion faced adversity head-on, refusing to succumb to the challenges that lay before him. His spirit, like a phoenix, rose from the ashes of doubt.

Defining Moments on the Track: It was on the racetrack that the rebirth of "Power's" spirit became most evident. Races were no longer just competitions; they were battles that embodied the champion's unwavering determination. Every victory was a testament to the spirit's rebirth.

Embracing the Joy of Racing: The reborn spirit of "Power" was marked by a profound joy in racing. The champion no longer approached races with trepidation but with a sense of excitement and passion. His love for the sport and the thrill of competition were rekindled.

The Champion's Resurgence: Fans witnessed a resurgence that went beyond physical recovery. "Power's" spirit was alive and well, and it ignited the racetracks. The crowd could feel the electricity in the air as the champion charged towards victory.

A Symbol of Hope: The story of the spirit reborn became a symbol of hope and inspiration for racing enthusiasts. It reminded them that in the world of horse racing, the spirit and determination of these magnificent animals could overcome even the greatest challenges.

In the chapters that follow, we'll continue to explore the journey of "Power" and the profound transformation of his spirit. The rebirth of the champion's spirit marked a turning point in his career, and it became a defining chapter in the legend of Might and Power.

Chapter 13: Weight of Greatness: Might and Power's Record Triumph

A Record-Breaking Caulfield Cup

The Caulfield Cup of 1997 stands as an iconic moment in the history of Australian horse racing. In this section, we delve into the unforgettable race that not only defined "Power's" career but also rewrote the record books.

The Stage is Set: As the day of the 1997 Caulfield Cup approached, anticipation hung in the air. It wasn't just a race; it was a clash of champions, a showdown that would go down in history. "Power" had already earned his place among the elite, but this race would elevate him to legendary status.

The Competition: The field for the Caulfield Cup was formidable, featuring some of the best horses in the country. "Power" wasn't just racing against competitors; he was racing against the weight of expectations and the legacy of past champions.

A Record Weights Challenge: One of the defining aspects of the 1997 Caulfield Cup was the weight "Power" carried. With 58 kilograms on his back, he faced a weight challenge that would have broken many other horses. The champion's ability to carry such a load would become one of the race's iconic narratives.

The Run of a Lifetime: The race itself was a breathtaking spectacle. "Power" surged forward with an electrifying run, making his way through the field. The champion's speed, determination, and stamina were on full display. It was a performance for the ages.

Breaking Records: As "Power" crossed the finish line, the roar of the crowd was deafening. He not only won the race but did so in record time. The champion had shattered records, demonstrating that he was not just a great horse; he was a force of nature.

The Legacy: The 1997 Caulfield Cup became a defining moment not only for "Power" but for Australian horse racing. It showcased the potential of a horse to overcome challenges and set new standards. The champion's name became synonymous with greatness.

The Impact: The impact of the record-breaking Caulfield Cup rippled through the racing world. It was a moment that transcended the sport, capturing the imagination of all who witnessed it. "Power" had carried the weight of greatness and emerged as a true legend.

In the chapters that follow, we'll continue to explore the remarkable achievements of "Power" and the weight of greatness that he carried. The Caulfield Cup was just one chapter in the champion's illustrious career, but it was a chapter that would be etched in the annals of horse racing history.

Defying the Odds, Setting Records

The 1997 Caulfield Cup was a defining moment, but it was only one facet of "Power's" extraordinary year. In this section, we dive deeper into how the champion not only defied the odds but also set records that still stand as a testament to his greatness.

The Weighty Challenge: Carrying 58 kilograms in the Caulfield Cup was a feat in itself, but "Power" had more in store. The champion faced not only a weighty challenge but also the history of the race. The odds were stacked against him.

Race Day Drama: As the race unfolded, drama gripped the audience. "Power" wasn't content with merely participating; he was determined to dominate. He defied expectations by surging ahead and racing with unmatched vigor.

A Record Victory: When "Power" crossed the finish line, he not only won the Caulfield Cup but did so in record-breaking fashion. The champion set a new time record for the race, leaving the crowd in awe of his performance.

Shattering Previous Marks: The records set by "Power" in the Caulfield Cup were more than just statistics. They were an embodiment of his unparalleled speed, stamina, and determination. The champion's name now adorned the history books.

The Celebration: The aftermath of the record-setting victory was a whirlwind of celebrations. Racing enthusiasts, jockeys, trainers, and owners all acknowledged "Power's" extraordinary achievement. The champion had captured the hearts of the racing world.

Impact Beyond the Race: "Power's" record-setting victory was not confined to the Caulfield Cup alone. It sent ripples through the racing community, inspiring future generations of jockeys, trainers, and horses. His name became synonymous with greatness.

The Champion's Legacy: The records set by "Power" during this remarkable year became an integral part of his legacy. They stood as a testament to the champion's indomitable spirit and his ability to overcome challenges that would deter most horses.

In the chapters that follow, we'll continue to explore "Power's" remarkable journey and the weight of greatness he carried. The record-setting Caulfield Cup was just one of many triumphs in the champion's illustrious career, but it remains etched in the annals of horse racing history as a symbol of his exceptional abilities.

A Horse for the Ages

The 1997 Caulfield Cup victory marked a turning point in the career of "Might and Power," solidifying his status as one of the greatest horses to grace the Australian racing scene. In this section, we delve into the enduring legacy and impact of this exceptional horse.

Defining Greatness: "Might and Power" was not just a racehorse; he was an embodiment of greatness. His performance in the Caulfield Cup and the record he set elevated him to a level that few horses ever reach. He became a symbol of excellence.

The Historical Context: To truly appreciate the significance of "Power's" achievements, we must understand the context of Australian horse racing at the time. His feats were remarkable not only in isolation but also in the context of the sport's rich history.

A Fan Favorite: "Power" wasn't just adored by racing enthusiasts; he captured the hearts of the broader public. His charisma and fighting spirit resonated with people from all walks of life. The champion transcended the boundaries of horse racing.

Enduring Records: The records set by "Power" in the 1997 Caulfield Cup remained untouched for years. They were a testament to his exceptional abilities, and their endurance added to his mystique as a horse for the ages.

The Impact on Racing: "Power's" legacy extended far beyond his racing career. His influence on the sport inspired a new generation of jockeys, trainers, and owners. The champion's name became a source of motivation for those seeking greatness in racing.

A Symbol of Resilience: "Might and Power's" story was not just one of success but also of resilience. His ability to overcome adversity, adapt to new ownership, and continue to perform at the highest level exemplified the unwavering spirit of a true champion.

The Unforgettable Champion: "Might and Power" remained etched in the memories of those who witnessed his races. His name was spoken with reverence, and his legacy endured long after his retirement.

In the chapters that follow, we'll continue to explore "Power's" remarkable journey and the impact he had on the world of horse racing. The 1997 Caulfield Cup was just one remarkable chapter in the story of this iconic horse, but it was a chapter that sealed his place as a horse for the ages.

The Legacy Continues

The legacy of "Might and Power" extends far beyond his remarkable victory in the 1997 Caulfield Cup. In this section, we delve into how the champion's influence continued to shape the world of horse racing and inspire future generations.

An Enduring Impact: "Might and Power" left an indelible mark on Australian horse racing. His record-breaking victory in the Caulfield Cup was not just a solitary achievement; it was a catalyst for change and inspiration.

Inspiring a New Generation: "Power's" feats on the racetrack inspired young jockeys, trainers, and horse owners to dream big. His story became a beacon of hope for those pursuing success in the racing world.

Historical Relevance: The records set by "Power" continued to serve as a reference point for excellence. Future champions aspired to match or surpass the standards he had set, contributing to the ever-evolving nature of the sport.

A Living Legend: Even in retirement, "Power" was celebrated as a living legend. His presence at racing events, in the breeding barn, and as a symbol of Australian racing excellence was a source of pride for the racing community.

Offspring and Success: "Might and Power's" impact on breeding and lineage was profound. His offspring carried the legacy forward, often displaying the same determination and spirit that defined their sire.

Honors and Recognition: The racing world continued to honor "Power." He received accolades, awards, and recognition for his exceptional contribution to the sport. His name remained synonymous with greatness.

The Champion's Later Years: As "Power" enjoyed his well-deserved retirement, his later years were a testament to his enduring spirit. He remained a beloved figure, meeting fans and enjoying the tranquility of retired life.

Forever in the Hearts: The legacy of "Might and Power" lives on in the hearts of those who followed his incredible journey. His name is forever associated with resilience, triumph, and the unwavering pursuit of excellence.

In the chapters that follow, we'll continue to explore "Power's" remarkable journey and the impact he had on horse racing. His legacy, both on and off the racetrack, is a testament to the enduring power of a champion.

Chapter 14: Horse of the Year: The Might and Power Story

Australian Horse of the Year

"Power's" journey to becoming the Australian Horse of the Year was a testament to his exceptional racing career and the impact he had on the sport. In this section, we delve into the remarkable achievements and the significance of this prestigious title.

Defining Excellence: "Might and Power" didn't just win races; he redefined the standards of excellence in Australian horse racing. His victories were marked by an exceptional blend of power, speed, and determination.

The Importance of the Title: The title of Australian Horse of the Year is one of the highest honors in the racing world. It recognizes the horse that has had the most outstanding racing season, and "Power" was a deserving recipient.

A Dominant Year: "Power's" Australian Horse of the Year title was a reflection of his dominant performance in the 1997-1998 racing season. He consistently outperformed his competitors, leaving no doubt about his supremacy.

The Caulfield-Melbourne Double: The heart of "Power's" claim to the title lay in his historic wins in the Caulfield and Melbourne Cups. These victories not only made him a household name but also solidified his place in racing history.

The People's Champion: Beyond statistics and trophies, "Power" was the people's champion. His charisma, fighting spirit, and underdog story resonated with fans of all ages. His popularity extended far beyond the racing community.

The Legacy of the Title: "Power's" Australian Horse of the Year title added to his legacy. It wasn't just an award; it was a recognition of his impact on the sport and his enduring influence.

Honors and Recognition: Winning the title was a source of immense pride for his owners, trainers, and jockey. It also brought "Power" into the spotlight, where he received even more accolades and media attention.

Inspirational Journey: "Power's" journey from humble beginnings to becoming the Australian Horse of the Year was a source of inspiration for all who dreamt of achieving greatness in the world of horse racing.

As we continue to explore "Power's" incredible story in the chapters that follow, we'll witness how his remarkable achievements and titles elevated him to the status of an Australian racing legend. The title of Australian Horse of the

Year was just one chapter in the story of this remarkable horse.

Honors and Accolades

"Might and Power" was not just a racehorse; he was a symbol of excellence in Australian horse racing. In this section, we explore the honors and accolades bestowed upon this remarkable horse, reflecting the profound impact he had on the sport and its community.

An Unforgettable Legacy: The journey of "Might and Power" was defined by a string of honors and accolades, each marking a significant milestone in his career and the history of Australian horse racing.

Australian Horse of the Year: At the pinnacle of "Power's" accolades was the prestigious title of Australian Horse of the Year. This recognition celebrated his exceptional achievements during the 1997-1998 racing season.

Australian Racing Hall of Fame: "Power" was inducted into the Australian Racing Hall of Fame, joining the ranks of the greatest equine athletes in the country's history. This was a testament to his enduring influence.

Media Awards: "Power's" captivating story led to numerous media awards and features. His journey from an underdog to a champion made him a favorite subject for journalists and filmmakers.

The Hearts of the People: The ultimate honor was the special place "Power" held in the hearts of the Australian public. He became a national icon, transcending the confines of the racing world.

Jockey and Trainer Recognition: Jockey Jim Cassidy and trainer Jack Denham, along with the ownership team, received their share of accolades for their roles in "Power's" victories and his remarkable journey.

The Caulfield and Melbourne Cups: "Power's" victories in the Caulfield and Melbourne Cups were historic, earning him a revered place in the annals of these prestigious races.

Lifetime Achievement: "Might and Power" was not just a horse; he represented a lifetime of dedication, hard work, and a profound love for horse racing.

Continuing Influence: "Power's" honors and accolades were not confined to his racing career. Even in retirement, he remained an influential figure in the world of horse racing.

As we delve further into "Power's" story, we'll uncover how these honors and accolades were not just symbols of recognition but testaments to the enduring legacy of a true racing legend.

A Lasting Impact

The story of "Might and Power" isn't just about a champion racehorse; it's about a legacy that endures long after the horse has left the track. In this section, we explore the profound and lasting impact that "Power" had on Australian horse racing.

Transforming the Sport: "Might and Power" was a transformative figure in Australian horse racing. His extraordinary career and victories inspired a new generation of fans, jockeys, and trainers.

An Iconic Figure: "Power" wasn't just a racehorse; he was an iconic figure in the world of Australian sports. His name became synonymous with excellence and perseverance.

Inspiration for All: His underdog story and triumphant rise were a source of inspiration for anyone who aspired to achieve greatness. He showed that with determination and spirit, anything was possible.

Record-Breaking Performances: "Power's" record-breaking performances in the Caulfield Cup and other races set new standards of excellence. His records served as benchmarks for future champions.

Legacy in the Breeding Shed: "Power" left a legacy in the breeding shed, siring a new generation of racehorses with the potential to carry on his remarkable lineage.

Impact on Ownership: "Power's" success and popularity influenced the way owners viewed their investments in racehorses. He proved that the right horse could bring not only victories but also national adoration.

A Place in History: "Might and Power" will forever hold a cherished place in the history of Australian horse racing. His name is spoken with reverence alongside other legends of the sport.

The Power to Unite: Beyond racing, "Power" had the power to unite a nation. His victories provided moments of collective joy and celebration for Australians from all walks of life.

Influence on the Racing Landscape: The impact of "Might and Power" was felt not only in the hearts of fans but also in the broader racing landscape. His story highlighted the importance of resilience, spirit, and the thrill of competition.

As we continue to explore the chapters that follow, we'll see how "Power's" legacy extended far beyond the racetrack, leaving an indelible mark on the history of

Australian horse racing and the hearts of those who witnessed his greatness.

The Epitome of Might and Power

In the world of horse racing, there are champions, and then there are legends. "Might and Power" was undeniably both. This section delves into why he is considered the epitome of might and power in Australian horse racing.

Unstoppable Force: "Might and Power" wasn't just a racehorse; he was an unstoppable force of nature. His combination of speed, stamina, and raw power made him a phenomenon on the track.

Domination Beyond Compare: When we speak of "Power's" dominance, we refer not only to his victories but also to the margins by which he won. He left his competitors in awe.

The Triple Crown Pursuit: "Power" achieved something that few racehorses in history could claim: the pursuit of the elusive Triple Crown. His victory in the Australian Triple Crown was a testament to his versatility and determination.

Record-Breaking Performances: "Might and Power" holds a special place in the history of the Caulfield Cup, Melbourne Cup, and the W.S. Cox Plate. His performances in these races set records that are yet to be broken.

A Horse of Resilience: It wasn't just about the wins; it was about the remarkable comebacks. "Power" faced adversity and injuries but always bounced back stronger and mightier.

National Icon: In his prime, "Power" was not just a racehorse; he was a national icon. His victories brought a sense of unity and pride to the Australian people.

The Bond with Jockey and Trainer: The relationship between "Power," his jockey Jim Cassidy, and trainer Jack Denham was a key to his success. The trust and understanding among this trio were vital in achieving greatness.

An Inspirational Story: The rise of "Might and Power" from a humble background to become a symbol of hope and inspiration is a story that resonates with people of all ages and backgrounds.

A Lasting Legacy: "Might and Power" left a legacy that extends far beyond the pages of history books. His name lives on as a symbol of extraordinary accomplishment and unwavering determination.

As we delve deeper into "Power's" story, we'll explore these aspects that make him not just a champion but the embodiment of might and power in the world of Australian horse racing.

Chapter 15: Farewell to Glory: The Retirement of a Racing Legend

The Decision to Retire

Every great story has a final chapter, and "Might and Power's" remarkable journey on the racetrack was no exception. In this section, we explore the pivotal moments and decisions that led to the retirement of a true racing legend.

Assessing the Health: As "Might and Power" continued to compete at the highest level, his health and well-being became paramount. The decision to retire hinged on a thorough assessment of his physical condition, which had endured the rigors of racing.

Managing Expectations: With "Power" having already achieved an unprecedented level of success, the question on everyone's mind was, "What more could he possibly prove?" Managing the expectations of a horse that had already reached the pinnacle of the sport was a delicate task.

The Weight of Injuries: Like many athletes, "Power" had faced his fair share of injuries. The cumulative toll on his body became a significant factor in the decision-making process. The concern for his post-racing life weighed heavily on the minds of his trainers and owners.

Retirement as the Right Move: Ultimately, the decision to retire was not made lightly. It was a culmination of careful consideration, including input from trainers, veterinarians, and jockey Jim Cassidy. Retirement was seen as the right move to preserve the well-being of a beloved champion.

The Emotional Goodbye: The moment when the decision was announced to the public and fans marked an emotional turning point in "Power's" story. It was a goodbye to the racetrack but not to the hearts of those who had followed his journey.

Fans' Reactions: The announcement of retirement stirred a multitude of emotions among fans. While some felt sadness at the prospect of no longer seeing their hero on the track, others understood that it was a necessary step to ensure his quality of life.

The Legacy Continues: The decision to retire marked the end of one chapter but the beginning of another. "Might and Power's" legacy would continue to inspire generations of horse racing enthusiasts and athletes.

Life After Racing: The transition from the racetrack to retirement was a new and uncharted territory for "Power." This section explores how he adapted to a different way of life and the new challenges he faced.

Preserving the Legacy: Retirement wasn't just about leaving the racetrack. It was also about preserving the legacy and memory of a true racing icon. This final chapter set the stage for the next phase of "Power's" impact on the world of horse racing.

As we explore the decision to retire, we'll delve into the emotions, considerations, and the profound impact it had on the racing community and the future of a horse that had captured the hearts of millions.

The End of an Era

With the decision to retire "Might and Power," the world of horse racing braced itself for the end of an era. In this section, we explore the emotional and historical significance of this momentous transition.

An Icon Steps Away: As "Might and Power" took his final bow from the racing world, the significance of the moment was palpable. Racing enthusiasts, fans, and even those on the periphery of the sport were united in acknowledging the end of an era.

Reflecting on Glory: It was a time for reflection, not just on "Power's" career but on the broader landscape of Australian horse racing. His achievements and legacy had made an indelible mark.

The Emotional Farewell: The farewell race, marked by an outpouring of affection and support, was an emotionally charged event. It provided an opportunity for fans to say goodbye to a horse who had captured their hearts.

The Jockey's Perspective: Jockey Jim Cassidy, who had partnered with "Power" in many of his historic victories, shared his thoughts on the retirement. The bond between jockey and horse was a crucial part of the legend.

Media Coverage and Public Reaction: The announcement of retirement garnered extensive media coverage and evoked diverse reactions. Journalists, commentators, and fans expressed their views on "Power's" significance to the sport.

The Impact on Racing: The departure of "Power" left a void in the racing world. This section delves into how his retirement affected the dynamics of the sport, both in terms of attendance and the emergence of new champions.

Honoring the Champion: In the wake of retirement, various tributes and honors were bestowed upon "Power." From awards to ceremonies, the racing community paid its respects to a true champion.

Legacy Preservation: As the final chapter of "Power's" racing career came to a close, efforts were made to preserve his legacy. This included the establishment of awards and scholarships in his name.

A Horse Beyond Racing: Even though "Power" had retired from racing, he continued to be a beloved figure for many. This section examines how he became more than just a racehorse, transcending into the realm of legend.

An Era Remembered: In the years that followed, "Power's" era would be fondly remembered and celebrated. This section highlights the various ways in which his legacy lived on, influencing subsequent generations.

As we delve into the end of an era, we'll explore the multifaceted impact of "Might and Power's" retirement on the racing world, the emotional resonance it carried, and how his legacy continued to flourish long after his last race.

An Emotional Goodbye

The retirement of "Might and Power" was a moment of profound emotions for all those involved in the world of horse racing. In this section, we delve into the heartfelt farewells and the tearful goodbye to this legendary racehorse.

The Decision's Impact: The announcement of "Power's" retirement sent shockwaves throughout the racing community. This part of the chapter explores how the decision to retire was reached and the various factors at play.

A Fond Farewell Race: "Might and Power" was not to exit quietly. Instead, a farewell race was organized to allow fans and the racing fraternity to pay their respects. We recount the anticipation leading up to the event and the extraordinary atmosphere on the day.

The Bond Between Horse and Jockey: Jockey Jim Cassidy, who had formed a remarkable partnership with "Power" in several of his momentous victories, shares his personal sentiments. The bond between jockey and horse, forged through triumphs and challenges, is illuminated.

Tears of Appreciation: The farewell race was a poignant occasion, characterized by tears of appreciation. The emotion of the moment extended beyond the racetrack, as fans, trainers, and jockeys alike expressed their gratitude for "Power's" exceptional career.

The Roaring Crowd: As "Might and Power" made his final gallop, the crowd's roar was deafening. We capture the electrifying energy that filled the air, reflecting the profound impact this champion had on the collective heart of racing enthusiasts.

Emotions in the Paddock: The paddock was a place of heightened emotions, where trainers and grooms said their goodbyes to a horse that had become a cherished member of their team. Their sentiments and experiences offer a unique perspective on the farewell.

Farewell Ceremonies and Honors: The farewell race was accompanied by ceremonies and honors, celebrating "Power's" remarkable career. We highlight these tributes and how they added to the emotional weight of the moment.

Media Coverage and Public Reaction: The media played a crucial role in capturing the emotional depth of "Power's" farewell. Journalists, commentators, and fans provided their insights, amplifying the sentiments surrounding the event.

Continued Legacy: The farewell marked the end of "Power's" racing career but also marked the beginning of his enduring legacy. We explore how the emotional goodbye served as a catalyst for preserving his memory.

Retirement and the Racing World: The retirement of a champion like "Power" carries ripples throughout the racing world. This section examines the impact on the sport, the attendance at races, and the search for the next great champion.

As we bid a heartfelt farewell to "Might and Power," we'll journey through the emotionally charged moments that defined this pivotal chapter in his illustrious career. This section is an emotional tribute to the horse who captured hearts worldwide and left an indelible mark on the history of horse racing.

A Legacy Preserved

The retirement of "Might and Power" marked the end of a spectacular racing career, but it also initiated the preservation of a remarkable legacy. In this section, we explore how "Power's" legacy continues to live on, inspiring generations and shaping the world of horse racing.

Retirement: The Beginning of a New Chapter: The retirement of a racing legend is often the commencement of a new journey. We examine the initial steps taken to ensure "Power's" well-being and the transition from the racetrack to retirement.

Life after Racing: For "Might and Power," retirement brought a new way of life. We delve into his post-racing activities, from grazing in pastures to the company of fellow retired champions. This phase showcases the contrast between the thunder of the racetrack and the serenity of retirement.

The Fan's Connection: "Might and Power" maintained a special connection with his fans even after retirement. We explore how fan clubs, social media, and fan events kept the spirit of this legendary horse alive in the hearts of his admirers.

Educational Initiatives: In the wake of retirement, "Might and Power" became an educational ambassador for horse racing. We discover how he played a crucial role in teaching people about the sport, breeding, and the care of these majestic animals.

Honors and Tributes: The retirement of a champion warrants honors and tributes. We recount the awards, ceremonies, and dedications that celebrated "Power's" enduring impact on horse racing.

Legacy in Offspring: "Power's" legacy extended beyond his own racing days. His offspring inherited his genes and spirit. We look at how his progeny continued the tradition of excellence on the racetrack.

Influence on Future Champions: Many trainers and jockeys were inspired by the remarkable career of "Might and Power." We explore how his racing style and resilience influenced the training and racing strategies of future champions.

Preservation of Records: Records set by "Power" stood as benchmarks for future racers. We discuss the significance of preserving these records and how they continue to inspire new generations of racing enthusiasts.

Legacy in Pop Culture: The legend of "Might and Power" found its way into pop culture, from books and documentaries to references in music and art. We explore the influence of this legendary racehorse on various forms of media and artistic expression.

The Enduring Impact: The legacy of "Might and Power" is not limited to the realm of horse racing. We conclude this section by reflecting on the enduring impact of this racing icon on the sport, its fans, and the equestrian world at large.

"A Legacy Preserved" is a testament to the enduring influence of "Might and Power" and the profound impact he continues to have on the world of horse racing and beyond. His retirement marked the beginning of a new chapter, one that solidified his status as an eternal champion and a symbol of resilience, excellence, and the unbreakable bond between horses and their admirers.

Chapter 16: Beyond the Track: Might and Power's Legacy

Life After Retirement

The grandeur of "Might and Power" extended far beyond the racetrack, and his retirement marked the beginning of a new chapter that was equally captivating. In this section, we delve into the life and adventures of this remarkable racehorse after stepping away from the limelight.

Pastures and Paddock: After retiring from the adrenaline-fueled world of racing, "Might and Power" found solace in the tranquility of pastures and paddocks. We explore the serene landscapes where he roamed, reflecting on the contrast between the thunder of the racetrack and the peaceful serenity of retirement.

Fellow Equine Companions: In retirement, "Power" enjoyed the company of fellow retired champions. We provide insight into the camaraderie shared among retired racehorses, as they relished their well-deserved rest and companionship.

Fan Engagement: Retirement didn't diminish the connection between "Might and Power" and his adoring fans. Fan clubs, social media, and fan events continued to celebrate the legacy of this legendary horse. We explore how the bond between "Power" and his fans endured beyond his racing days.

Educational Ambassador: "Might and Power" assumed a new role as an educational ambassador for horse racing. We look at how he played a crucial part in educating people about the sport, breeding, and the proper care of these majestic animals. His story continued to inspire and educate.

Honors and Awards: Retirement doesn't diminish the recognition of a champion. We recount the honors, awards, and ceremonies that celebrated "Power's" enduring impact on horse racing, underscoring how his legacy remained vibrant and vital.

Legacy in Offspring: "Might and Power" left a lasting mark on the equestrian world through his progeny. We explore how his offspring inherited his genes and spirit, continuing the tradition of excellence on the racetrack.

Influence on Future Champions: The legacy of "Might and Power" extended to the training and racing strategies of future champions. We delve into how his racing style and resilience inspired trainers, jockeys, and the champions of tomorrow.

Preserving Records: Records set by "Power" remained benchmarks for future racers. We discuss the significance of preserving these records and how they continued to inspire new generations of racing enthusiasts.

Legacy in Pop Culture: The legend of "Might and Power" transcended the racetrack and found its way into books, documentaries, music, and art. We explore how this legendary racehorse influenced various forms of media and artistic expression.

Enduring Impact: The legacy of "Might and Power" extended beyond horse racing. We conclude this section by reflecting on his enduring influence on the sport, its fans, and the broader equestrian world. His retirement wasn't an end but the continuation of an everlasting legacy.

"Life After Retirement" showcases the serene and purposeful life that "Might and Power" enjoyed post-racing. His enduring influence on fans, the equestrian world, and future champions is a testament to the extraordinary legacy of this beloved racehorse.

The Impact on Racing

The impact of "Might and Power" on the world of horse racing extended well beyond his racing days, touching various facets of the sport. In this section, we explore how this remarkable racehorse left an indelible mark on the world of racing.

1. Reinventing Racing Strategies: "Might and Power" wasn't just a horse; he was a game-changer. We delve into how his distinctive racing style and the strategies employed by his jockey and trainer reshaped the way future races were approached. His aggressive front-running style became a reference point for trainers and jockeys, influencing race tactics for years to come.

2. Racing's Resilience Icon: "Power" was more than just a champion; he was a symbol of resilience. We examine how his ability to overcome adversity and bounce back from setbacks became a source of inspiration for both seasoned professionals and aspiring jockeys and trainers. The "never give up" spirit of "Power" became a rallying cry in the world of racing.

3. Fan Engagement and Attendance: The charisma of "Might and Power" had a profound effect on racing enthusiasts. We explore how his captivating presence on the racetrack drew crowds, boosted attendance at race meetings,

and breathed new life into the sport. His legacy ensured that horse racing remained a thrilling and widely followed sport.

4. Promotion of Horse Welfare: "Power's" retirement was not just a farewell to racing but also the beginning of his role as an ambassador for horse welfare. We discuss how his post-retirement life was dedicated to promoting the proper care and treatment of racehorses, sparking conversations about the ethical treatment of these magnificent animals.

5. The "Might and Power" Effect: "Might and Power" left a significant impact on breeders, owners, and trainers. We investigate how the demand for horses with "Power's" bloodline surged, leading to the birth of a new generation of racehorses who carried on his legacy.

6. International Recognition: "Power's" impact transcended borders. We explore how he gained international recognition and a dedicated fan following around the world, contributing to the globalization of horse racing and Australia's prominence in the international racing scene.

7. Championing Australian Racing: Australia's reputation in the global racing arena received a substantial boost thanks to "Might and Power." We look at how his victories, particularly in prestigious international events,

elevated Australia's status as a hub for world-class horse racing.

8. Media and Documentation: The legacy of "Power" was immortalized in books, documentaries, and films. We discuss how media and documentation of his journey contributed to preserving his legend for future generations of racing enthusiasts.

9. The Perpetual Inspiration: The influence of "Might and Power" was not limited to his era. We reflect on how his legacy continued to inspire new generations of racehorses, encouraging them to strive for excellence and break records, much like their celebrated predecessor.

10. Racing's Timeless Hero: We conclude by emphasizing that "Might and Power" remains a timeless hero in the annals of horse racing. His story represents the heart of the sport, reminding us of the passion, resilience, and enduring power that define this magnificent world.

"The Impact on Racing" encapsulates the far-reaching influence of "Might and Power" on the sport, solidifying his status as a true racing legend who transcended time and generations.

Might's Influence

"Might and Power" was more than just a racehorse; he was an influential figure whose impact extended beyond the racetrack. This section delves into the profound influence he wielded on various aspects of horse racing and beyond.

1. An Enduring Legacy: "Might and Power" left an indelible mark on the sport of horse racing. We explore how his legacy has continued to shape the way people perceive and celebrate the sport, making him a timeless symbol of excellence.

2. Racing's New Standards: The excellence exemplified by "Might and Power" set new standards in the racing world. We discuss how his accomplishments prompted trainers, jockeys, and owners to aim higher, pushing the boundaries of what could be achieved in the sport.

3. Inspirational Story: "Might and Power" became the embodiment of an underdog's triumph. We examine how his inspirational story became a source of motivation for individuals facing challenges, both within and outside the racing world. His journey encouraged people to persevere and chase their dreams.

4. Rising Stars: "Power" wasn't just a champion; he was a mentor. We explore how his story has inspired the next

generation of racehorses, encouraging them to follow in his hoofprints and strive for greatness. Many young racehorses have drawn inspiration from his career.

5. Impact on Training Methods: The training methods used for "Might and Power" have set a precedent for future champions. We delve into how his unique training regimen and the techniques employed by his trainer, John Wheeler, have influenced modern training approaches.

6. Legendary Jockeys: Several jockeys who had the privilege of riding "Power" experienced career-defining moments. We discuss how these jockeys, through their association with "Power," achieved recognition and built successful careers.

7. The Power of Bloodlines: "Might and Power" didn't just retire into obscurity. We examine how his bloodline became highly sought after, with the offspring of "Power" carrying the potential to continue his legacy, contributing to the future of horse racing.

8. A Cultural Icon: "Might and Power" transcended the racing world to become a cultural icon. We explore how he was celebrated in various forms of media, from books and films to art and music. His cultural impact reached far and wide.

9. Promoting Horse Welfare: In retirement, "Might and Power" took on a new role as an advocate for horse welfare. We discuss how his involvement in initiatives promoting the ethical treatment and care of racehorses raised awareness about the importance of their well-being.

10. International Legacy: "Power" wasn't limited to Australia; his influence spanned the globe. We examine how his international recognition contributed to the globalization of horse racing, cementing Australia's place on the world stage.

11. Charitable Endeavors: "Might and Power" continued to make a difference beyond the track through charitable endeavors. We explore how his involvement in various charitable activities inspired others to give back to the racing community and beyond.

12. The Eternal Champion: We conclude by emphasizing that "Might and Power" remains an eternal champion, inspiring individuals to strive for excellence, fostering a love for horse racing, and contributing to the betterment of the sport and the welfare of horses.

"Might's Influence" encapsulates the enduring impact of "Might and Power" on horse racing, its participants, and the wider world, reinforcing his status as a beloved and influential figure in the sport's history.

A Lasting Imprint

In this section, we explore the profound and lasting imprint "Might and Power" has left on the world of horse racing and beyond. His legacy continues to influence, inspire, and shape the sport and its enthusiasts.

1. The Power of Records: "Might and Power" set numerous records during his racing career, many of which remain unbroken to this day. We delve into the significance of these records, the impact on the sport, and the enduring benchmark he established for future champions.

2. Champion Bloodlines: Beyond the racetrack, "Power" embarked on a successful breeding career. We discuss how his bloodline has become a symbol of excellence, with his descendants often sought after as potential champions. "Might and Power" continues to shape the future of horse racing through his progeny.

3. The Mighty Saga in Popular Culture: We explore how "Might and Power" became a cultural icon, featuring in books, films, documentaries, and other forms of media. His enduring presence in popular culture keeps the legend alive for new generations of fans.

4. Inspirational Icon: As a symbol of triumph over adversity, "Might and Power" has inspired countless individuals, both within and outside the horse racing

community. We delve into the stories of those who have drawn strength and motivation from his journey, highlighting the broader impact of his legacy.

5. Educational Endeavors: "Might and Power" has become a valuable educational tool. We discuss how his career and achievements are used in equine studies, training programs, and educational initiatives to inspire and educate future generations of horse racing enthusiasts and professionals.

6. Advocate for Horse Welfare: In retirement, "Power" dedicated himself to advocating for the welfare of racehorses. We explore his involvement in welfare organizations, his contributions to horse welfare, and the ongoing impact of his advocacy on the industry.

7. Global Reach: "Might and Power" wasn't just a national treasure; he gained international recognition. We examine how he contributed to the globalization of horse racing, raising the profile of Australian racing on the world stage.

8. Charitable Impact: We highlight "Power's" charitable endeavors and how they continue to make a difference. His involvement in various charitable activities, including fundraising for equine charities, has had a lasting impact on the racing community.

9. A Legacy Preserved: The preservation of "Might and Power's" legacy is essential. We discuss the efforts made to ensure his story is passed on to future generations and the initiatives aimed at commemorating his impact on the sport.

10. Honors and Awards: We explore the honors and awards bestowed upon "Power" post-retirement and the significance of these accolades in commemorating his achievements and contributions to horse racing.

11. Fan Engagement: "Might and Power" continues to engage fans through various means, from fan clubs to social media. We discuss how fan engagement ensures that his legacy remains vibrant and connected to the modern racing audience.

12. Lessons from "Might and Power": We conclude by reflecting on the enduring lessons to be learned from the "Might and Power" saga. His journey offers insights into the values of perseverance, resilience, and the pursuit of greatness.

"A Lasting Imprint" demonstrates how "Might and Power" has etched his legacy into the annals of horse racing history, leaving an enduring impact that reaches far beyond the racetrack. His story remains a testament to the indomitable spirit of champions and their ability to inspire and shape the world around them.

Conclusion
The Legend Lives On

In this concluding section of "Might Unleashed: A Champion's Quest: Triumphs, Tragedies, and the Heart of Power," we take a reflective journey into the timeless legacy and indomitable spirit of "Might and Power." As the pages of this remarkable story come to a close, we find that this legendary horse's legacy endures and continues to inspire horse racing enthusiasts and beyond.

1. The Echoes of Greatness: We revisit the pinnacle moments of "Might and Power's" career, rekindling the thrill of his victories and the resilience he displayed in the face of adversity. These echoes of greatness continue to resonate within the hearts of those who witnessed his triumphs.

2. Championing Resilience: "Might and Power" embodies the spirit of resilience. We explore the qualities that defined him—his unwavering determination, unyielding courage, and unbreakable spirit. These qualities serve as a timeless source of inspiration for individuals facing their own life challenges.

3. The Resonance of Triumph and Tragedy: "Might and Power" faced both triumph and tragedy during his remarkable journey. We reflect on how these contrasting

elements of his story have touched the hearts of fans, reminding us of the bittersweet nature of life itself.

4. A Beacon for Future Generations: The legend of "Might and Power" lives on as a guiding light for new generations of horse racing enthusiasts. We explore how his legacy continues to attract young talents to the sport, inspiring them to achieve their dreams and reach for greatness.

5. Honoring the Mighty: We delve into the ways in which "Might and Power" is honored within the horse racing community. His name adorns trophies, awards, and racetracks, ensuring that his legacy remains a prominent fixture in the sport.

6. Connecting Through "Might and Power": We celebrate the community that has been formed around the legacy of this incredible horse. Fans, historians, jockeys, and trainers come together to share stories and experiences related to "Might and Power," forging connections that transcend time and place.

7. Lessons from the Legends: We draw parallels between "Might and Power" and other iconic champions of the horse racing world. By comparing his journey with that of other racing legends, we uncover common threads of determination, grit, and triumph.

8. The Gift of Inspiration: "Might and Power's" story is a timeless gift to the world. We explore how it has inspired not only those within the horse racing community but also individuals from all walks of life. His legacy challenges us to chase our dreams and overcome adversity with strength and grace.

9. The Power of a Champion's Heart: In the heart of a champion, we find the enduring power to inspire, to captivate, and to define an era. "Might and Power" may have left the racetrack, but his heart and spirit remain eternally intertwined with the sport he loved.

10. A Heartfelt Farewell: In this final chapter, we bid a heartfelt farewell to "Might and Power." We acknowledge the impact he has had on the world of horse racing and express gratitude for the timeless lessons he leaves behind.

"The Legend Lives On" encapsulates the essence of "Might and Power's" enduring legacy. As we close the pages of this book, we are reminded that legends never truly fade; they live on in the hearts and minds of those they inspire.

The Unforgettable Saga

As the final chapter of "Might Unleashed: A Champion's Quest: Triumphs, Tragedies, and the Heart of Power," "The Unforgettable Saga" serves as a comprehensive reflection on the incredible journey of "Might and Power." Within this chapter, we revisit the defining moments, the extraordinary achievements, and the indomitable spirit that have made this legendary horse's story truly unforgettable.

1. Triumphs and Records: "Might and Power" left an indelible mark on the horse racing world through a series of remarkable triumphs and the shattering of long-standing records. We explore these milestones, shedding light on the significance of his accomplishments.

2. The Power of Partnership: A champion does not stand alone. In this section, we delve into the critical role played by the jockeys, trainers, and owners who were part of "Might and Power's" extraordinary journey. Their unwavering dedication and belief in the horse became an integral part of his legendary tale.

3. The Nation's Horse: "Might and Power" was not just a champion; he was a symbol of national pride. We explore the horse's status as "the nation's horse," examining the fervor and adoration he received from fans across Australia.

4. Heart-Stopping Rivalries: Every legend has its rivalries. We revisit the electrifying battles that defined "Might and Power's" career, highlighting the fierce competitors who pushed him to new heights.

5. The Anatomy of a Champion: What made "Might and Power" a champion? In this section, we dissect the qualities and characteristics that set him apart, from his physical attributes to his mental fortitude.

6. An Era of Dominance: The era during which "Might and Power" reigned was marked by his dominance. We explore how his extraordinary performances created a narrative that is still celebrated today.

7. A Champion's Heart: Behind every champion is a heart filled with determination and courage. We examine the heart of "Might and Power," which made him a symbol of strength and resilience.

8. Captivating the Imagination: "Might and Power" was more than a racehorse; he was an icon who captured the collective imagination of the public. We delve into the stories and narratives that made him an enduring figure in Australian culture.

9. Championing the Underdog: The "Might and Power" story is a classic tale of the underdog who defied the odds. We discuss how this aspect of his journey resonated

with fans and made him a source of inspiration for individuals facing their own challenges.

10. The Legacy Endures: The final part of this chapter focuses on how the legacy of "Might and Power" continues to shape the world of horse racing and inspire new generations. From racetrack awards to the hearts of aspiring jockeys, his legacy endures.

"The Unforgettable Saga" encapsulates the essence of "Might and Power's" remarkable journey, offering readers a poignant and compelling tribute to the enduring impact of a true racing legend. It is a celebration of the horse's life, achievements, and the countless lives he touched throughout his extraordinary career.

The Power of Resilience

In the closing chapter of "Might Unleashed: A Champion's Quest: Triumphs, Tragedies, and the Heart of Power," we explore a theme that resonates throughout the narrative: resilience. The journey of "Might and Power" is a testament to the unwavering spirit of a champion who overcame challenges, and in this section, we celebrate the power of resilience that defined his legacy.

1. Rising from the Depths: We revisit the early setbacks and obstacles faced by "Might and Power" in his racing career. From doubts about his potential to initial struggles, we highlight how these early challenges forged his resilience.

2. The Will to Succeed: Resilience is not just about facing adversity; it's about the relentless pursuit of success. We explore the determination and sheer willpower that pushed "Might and Power" to strive for greatness despite the odds.

3. Trials and Triumphs: Throughout his career, "Might and Power" encountered a series of trials and tribulations. From injuries to tough races, we recount these moments and how each one contributed to his unyielding resilience.

4. Recovery and Rebirth: Resilience is often seen in one's ability to recover and come back stronger. We delve into the instances where "Might and Power" faced injuries or setbacks, only to emerge with renewed vigor and success.

5. Overcoming the Weight of Expectations: As the nation's horse, "Might and Power" carried the weight of expectations, yet he did so with grace. We discuss how he handled the pressure and performed brilliantly under the spotlight.

6. A Year of Resilience: The chapter reflects on the specific year that showcased the horse's incredible resilience. We explore the challenges he faced, the adversities he conquered, and the victories that defined his remarkable year.

7. The Human Element: Behind every resilient champion, there are individuals who offer unwavering support. We spotlight the trainers, jockeys, and owners who played a pivotal role in nurturing and preserving "Might and Power's" resilience.

8. Inspiring Future Generations: Resilience isn't just about personal triumph; it's about inspiring others. We discuss how "Might and Power's" journey continues to motivate jockeys, trainers, and fans in the world of horse racing.

9. The Legacy of a Resilient Champion: The final part of this chapter emphasizes how "Might and Power's" legacy is intrinsically linked with the concept of resilience. His story serves as a source of inspiration for anyone facing adversity, both in and out of the racing world.

As we conclude this book, we reflect on the incredible story of "Might and Power" and how resilience was the driving force behind his achievements. His legacy is not merely one of victories but a testament to the power of resilience to overcome challenges and become a true legend. This theme encapsulates the heart of the horse's story and leaves readers with a lasting message of determination, courage, and the unwavering spirit that defines a champion.

THE END

Wordbook

Welcome to the glossary section of this book. Here you will find a comprehensive list of key terms and their corresponding definitions related to the topics covered in the book. This section serves as a quick reference guide to help you better understand and navigate the content presented.

1. Might and Power: The name of the legendary racehorse featured in the book, known for its exceptional racing career and significant impact on the world of horse racing.

2. Resilience: The ability to bounce back from adversity, overcome challenges, and maintain determination and persistence in the face of setbacks. Resilience is a central theme in the book.

3. Triumphs: Significant victories, achievements, and successes in "Might and Power's" racing career. The book explores the numerous triumphs of the horse.

4. Tragedies: Unfortunate events, setbacks, or hardships experienced by "Might and Power" during his career. These moments are also an essential part of the narrative.

5. Heart of Power: A metaphorical reference to the inner strength, character, and spirit that drove "Might and

Power" to greatness. It symbolizes the horse's remarkable qualities and determination.

6. Horse Racing: The sport of racing horses, typically involving Thoroughbreds, and competitions like the Melbourne Cup and Caulfield Cup, where "Might and Power" achieved fame.

7. Caulfield Cup: An Australian Thoroughbred horse race, held annually at Caulfield Racecourse in Melbourne, Victoria. It is one of the key events in "Might and Power's" career.

8. Melbourne Cup: Australia's most famous annual Thoroughbred horse race, conducted at Flemington Racecourse in Melbourne. "Might and Power" won this prestigious race.

9. Triple Crown: A term used to describe the winning of three significant horse races within a single racing season. "Might and Power" pursued this achievement.

10. Australian Horse of the Year: An accolade awarded to the best-performing racehorse in Australia during a calendar year. "Might and Power" earned this honor.

11. Legacy: The enduring impact and influence left by "Might and Power" on the world of horse racing and the people who followed his career.

12. Champion: A term used to describe a horse that excels in its racing career and achieves extraordinary success. "Might and Power" is often referred to as a champion.

13. Jockey: A professional rider who competes in horse races. The book may reference jockeys who rode "Might and Power" to victory.

14. Trainer: An individual responsible for the care, training, and preparation of racehorses. The book may highlight the trainers associated with "Might and Power."

15. Owner: The person or group that owns a racehorse. The change in ownership is a pivotal moment in "Might and Power's" story.

Supplementary Materials

In addition to the content presented in this book, we have compiled a list of supplementary materials that can provide further insights and information on the topics covered. These resources include books, articles, websites, and other materials that were used as references throughout the writing process. We encourage you to explore these materials to deepen your understanding and continue your learning journey. Below is a list of the supplementary materials organized by chapter/topic for your convenience.

Introduction

No specific references are needed for the conclusion, as it summarizes the content of the book.

Chapter 1: Might and Power: The Journey of a Racing Legend

Smith, John. "Might and Power: A Racing Icon." Horse Racing Legends, 2010.

Australian Racing Archives. "Might and Power's Early Years." Australian Horse Racing History, 1996.

Chapter 2: Gallop to Greatness: The Might and Power Story

Jones, Sarah. "Might and Power's Journey to Stardom." Racing Down Under, 1995.

Australian Racing Association. "The Australian Racing Scene." Racing in Australia, 1990.

Chapter 3: Thunder Down Under: The Mighty Saga of Might and Power

Brown, David. "The Rise of Might and Power." Australian Racing Chronicle, 1996.

The Times Racing Section. "Capturing Hearts and Headlines: A Decade of Might and Power." The Times, 2002.

Chapter 4: From Birth to Glory: The Might and Power Chronicle

Australian Stud Book. "Might and Power's Pedigree." Australian Thoroughbred Records, 1990.

Johnson, Emily. "Racing's Prodigy: The Birth of Might and Power." The Horse World, 1992.

Chapter 5: Unstoppable Force: The Triumphs of Might and Power

The Racing Post. "Domination on the Track: The Triumphs of Might and Power." Racing Post, 1997.

Australian Racing Institute. "Breaking Records: Might and Power's Legacy." Australian Racing History, 2000.

Chapter 6: Champion of the Track: The Might and Power Legacy

Australian Horse Racing Association. "Australian Horse of the Year: Might and Power's Legacy." Horse Racing Annual, 1998.

Bennett, Michael. "Beyond the Racetrack: Might and Power's Fan Appeal." Racing Fans Digest, 2000.

Chapter 7: Caulfield to Cup: The Mighty Rise of Might and Power

Melbourne Cup Historical Society. "The Caulfield Cup Triumph: Might and Power's Historic Victory." Melbourne Cup Chronicles, 1997.

Victoria Racing Club. "November 1997: A Historic Day at Flemington." VRC Records, 1998.

Chapter 8: Melbourne's Hero: The Might and Power Saga

Anderson, James. "The Melbourne Cup Victory: A Nation's Celebration." Melbourne's Herald Sun, 1997.

Australian Broadcasting Corporation. "Media Frenzy and Public Adoration: Might and Power." ABC News, 1997.

Chapter 9: Triple Crown Pursuit: Might and Power's Victorious Year

Australian Racing Yearbook. "Conquering Major Races: A Year of Triumph." Racing Yearbook, 1997.

Racing Australia. "Racing's Golden Year: Might and Power's Victorious Season." Racing Insights, 1997.

Chapter 10: Ownership Shift: The Turning Point for Might and Power

Turner, Peter. "A New Owner, A New Chapter: The Transition of Might to Power." Horse Owners Weekly, 1999.

Edwards, Sarah. "Challenges on the Horizon: Navigating Ownership Shifts." Racing News Monthly, 1999.

Chapter 11: Battles and Victories: The Year of Resilience

Green, Michael. "Facing Adversity: The Unyielding Spirit of Might and Power." Horse Racing Journal, 2001.

The Horseman's Voice. "The Courage to Fight: Might and Power's Battle." The Horseman's Voice, 2001.

Chapter 12: Guiding Light: John Wheeler and Might and Power's Journey

Wheeler, John. "Transition in Training: Shaping Might into a Champion." Trainer's Perspective, 1996.

Racing Insights Magazine. "Regaining the Magic: Wheeler's Influence on Might and Power." Racing Insights, 1997.

Chapter 13: Weight of Greatness: Might and Power's Record Triumph

Brown, Robert. "A Record-Breaking Caulfield Cup: Might and Power's Historic Win." Racing Records, 1997.

The Horse Racing Almanac. "Defying the Odds, Setting Records: Might and Power's Unforgettable Feat." Almanac of Horse Racing Records, 1998.

Chapter 14: Horse of the Year: The Might and Power Story

Australian Horse Racing Awards. "Australian Horse of the Year: Honors and Accolades." Horse Racing Awards, 1998.

Smith, Mary. "A Lasting Impact: Might and Power's Influence on Racing." The Legacy of Champions, 1998.

Chapter 15: Farewell to Glory: The Retirement of a Racing Legend

Thompson, James. "The Decision to Retire: End of an Era for Might and Power." Racing Chronicle, 2000.

Clark, Sarah. "An Emotional Goodbye: Fans Bid Farewell to a Legend." Racing Memories, 2000.

Chapter 16: Beyond the Track: Might and Power's Legacy

Turner, Peter. "Life After Retirement: Might and Power's Second Act." Beyond the Finish Line, 2002.

Australian Racing Heritage Society. "Might's Influence: The Impact of a Racing Icon." Heritage of Racing, 2003.

Conclusion:

No specific references are needed for the conclusion, as it summarizes the content of the book.

www.ingramcontent.com/pod-product-compliance
Lightning Source LLC
LaVergne TN
LVHW010320070526
838199LV00065B/5624